S/NVQ
ssessor
andbook

for Children's Care, Learning & Development

Kelly Hill

www.harcourt.co.uk
✓ Free online support
✓ Useful weblinks
✓ 24 hour online ordering

01865 888118

Heinemann
From Harcourt

Heinemann Educational Publishers
Halley Court, Jordan Hill, Oxford OX2 8EJ
Part of Harcourt Education
Heinemann is the registered trademark of Harcourt Education Limited

First published 2007

10 09 08 07 06
10 9 8 7 6 5 4 3 2 1

British Library Cataloguing in Publication Data is available from the British Library on request.

13-digit ISBN: 978 0 435402 23 5

In House Team
Managing Editor: Faye Cheeseman
Publisher: Beth Howard
Design: Georgia Bushell
Production: Jamie Copping

Copyedited by Tasha Goddard
Designed by Kamae Design
Typeset by TexTech International, Private Ltd
Original illustrations © Harcourt Education Limited, 2006
Illustrated by TexTech International, Private Ltd & TekArt, Surrey
Cover design by Wooden Ark Studio, Leeds
Printed in the UK by CPI Bath
Cover photo: © Harcourt Education Ltd/Jules Selmes/
Picture research: Cath Bevan

Websites

Please note that the examples of websites suggested in this book were up to date at the time of writing. It is essential for tutors to preview each site before using it to ensure that the URL is still accurate and the content is appropriate. We suggest that tutors bookmark useful sites and consider enabling students to access them through the school or college intranet.

About the author

Kelly Hill has been working in the early years and childcare sector for over 12 years, from nursery nursing to running her own successful early years training company. While running the training company, Kelly gained three business awards – New Business Start-up of the Year 2004, Young Entrepreneur of the Year 2004 and Business of the Year 2005.

Kelly has worked as an assessor, internal verifier and external verifier for a number of awarding bodies. As a freelance training consultant she has advised many centres on the development of their awards, supporting them to gain scheme approval and developing quality assurance schemes.

Kelly is now working as a freelance consultant and writer for a range of organisations, while being mum to her young family.

Contents

Acknowledgements   vi

Introduction   vii

Chapter 1
The S/NVQ for Children's Care, Learning and Development   1

Chapter 2
Supporting candidates   35

Chapter 3
Assessment processes   57

Chapter 4
The A1 and A2 awards   87

Chapter 5
Developing reflective practice   113

Chapter 6
Gathering evidence for the S/NVQ for Children's Care,
Learning and Development   123

Useful resources   161

Suggested solutions   163

Glossary   187

Index   191

Acknowledgements

I would like to start by thanking all those professionals who have given their advice and expertise for this book, and thanks to Beth Howard for her guidance and encouragement throughout.

I would also like to thank my husband Keith for his love, support and belief in me, and for nodding in all the right places!

And big hugs to my two beautiful girls for just being themselves!

The author and publisher would like to thank the following individuals and organisations for permission to reproduce photographs:

Alamy p104, 115, 123; Bubbles p83; Corbis/zefa/Grace p1; educationphotos.co.uk/walmsley p43(middle); Getty Images/PhotoDisc p43(bottom); Harcourt Education Ltd/Gareth Boden p3, 19; Harcourt Education Ltd/Jules Selmes p12, 17, 25, 47, 68, 90, 128, 130, 131, 133, 137, 142, 146, 150, 155, 158; Masterfile p113; Photofusion p6, 14, 38, 43(top), 45, 57, 111; Photos.com p35, 36, 87, 124.

Every effort has been made to contact copyright holders of material reproduced in this book. Any omissions will be rectified in subsequent printings if notice is given to the publishers.

Introduction

Welcome to this Assessor Handbook for Children's Care, Learning and Development (CCLD). In reading this handbook, you are probably preparing to work within the training sector, working with S/NVQ CCLD candidates. This book is aimed at helping you to support your candidates as they work towards gaining their CCLD qualification, and will be of use to you whether you are new to the assessment process, or are updating your skills in light of the changes in standards. Whatever level you are at, this handbook will offer you advice, information and guidance to support you in your role as assessor. It is not assumed that you have prior knowledge of S/NVQs, so if you are new to this qualification as well as the assessor role you will find this handbook of particular help.

Assessing the S/NVQ process for any award requires dedication, experience of the award and a passion to help others succeed in their chosen career. By becoming an assessor of the CCLD award, it is likely that you have made a rewarding career working with children and young people and now have the desire to help others achieve their goals and aspirations in the childcare sector. Being able to pass on your experience and knowledge is invaluable to candidates as they begin their career and by offering your help, guidance and support, you can give a helping hand in shaping the childcare workforce.

This book will provide you with practical tips and information on how to encourage, train and assess your candidates through their award, while helping you through your own training towards becoming an assessor. It is a comprehensive guide to the knowledge you need to become a competent and efficient assessor.

Each chapter covers a specific topic with in-depth information designed to allow you to dip in and out of the chapters as you wish, and continue to refer back to various topics as you work with your candidates.

- Chapter 1 acts as an introduction to the CCLD National Occupational Standards (NOS), helping you to understand how to effectively use the NOS and the importance of the Principles and Values within the sector.

- Chapter 2 looks more in-depth at the work of the assessor and how your role will develop. You will consider how to build relationships with your candidates and support those who may have additional needs.

- Chapter 3 addresses the assessment processes you will use to assess your candidates' competence, and helps you to learn how to plan, carry out and judge assessment opportunities and give feedback to your candidates. This chapter also looks at e-portfolios and how they can be used.

- Chapter 4 will help you to understand the A1 and A2 awards, looking at the requirements of the NOS and where quality assurance and standardisation fits into the NVQ.

- Chapter 5 encourages you to consider your work as an assessor, and reflect on your practice. It will demonstrate how to develop reflective skills and use reflection to challenge existing practice.

- Chapter 6, the final chapter within this handbook, demonstrates assessment opportunities and provides examples of how you might gather evidence for the CCLD NOS.

Features of this book

As you work your way through this handbook, you will come across a number of features that are designed to encourage you to reflect on your experiences and knowledge, and to support you in putting theory into practice. They will encourage you to research from a variety of media, including governmental legislation and assessment documentation. The features you will find within this handbook are:

- **Case studies** are scenarios intended to illustrate specific points and to help you to explore key issues. These will encourage you to apply your knowledge and to consider alternative ways of working.

- **Check it out features** are information boxes that will direct you to details of important documents and sources of key information.

- **Over to you!** activities help you engage with what you have learnt or read and encourage you to relate the knowledge within this book to your work situation. Suggested solutions are often provided at the back of the book.

- **Keys to good practice** are useful tips and practical ways of working within best practice guidelines.

- **Key terms** provide descriptions of important terms. The key terms are also provided, in alphabetical order, in the glossary at the back of the book.

- **Check your understanding** questions are provided at the end of each chapter and are aimed at helping you recap what you have just read or learnt.

These features are designed to get you thinking about how theory and practice link, and how to improve your current practice. Reading through the case studies and answering the questions will allow you to look at your stronger and weaker areas, as well as ensuring you have fully understood the text or the subject you have just read.

Documents you will need

Throughout this handbook, reference will be made to particular documents, and you will find it beneficial to obtain copies of these.

- CCLD National Occupational Standards
- Joint Awarding Body Guidance for S/NVQs and VQs in Children's Care, Learning and Development.
- Joint Awarding Body Guidance on Internal Verification of S/NVQs
- The S/NVQ Code of Practice
- The Green Paper – Every Child Matters
- The Children's Workforce Strategy
- The Lead Professional Good Practice Guidance
- The Common Core of Skills and Knowledge
- CCLD Assessment Strategy

You will find out where to obtain these documents within the specific chapters of the handbook.

I hope that you enjoy reading and using this handbook, and trust that you will find it a valuable tool as you work towards becoming a qualified S/NVQ assessor.

Chapter 1

The S/NVQ for Children's Care, Learning and Development

Introduction

Over the years, the National Occupational Standards (NOS) for the childcare sector have been developed, resulting in the current S/NVQ for Children's Care, Learning and Development (CCLD). As an assessor of these awards, you need to be familiar with the content and layout of the NOS and use them as a working tool to support your candidates' learning. You will find the information within this chapter relevant to you whether you are a new assessor working within the NOS for the first time or an experienced assessor making the transition from Early Years Care and Education (EYCE) to the new NOS. You will consider how the CCLD S/NVQ fits in with recent government legislation, as well as the role it plays in developing an integrated workforce within the childcare sector. This chapter will encourage you to find similarities and differences between the old and revised NOS and to think about why these changes have been made. It is important, therefore, that you have a copy of both the EYCE and CCLD NOS for Levels 2 and 3. You will also look at the Principles and Values of the sector and consider how these will impact on your own practice, as well as that of your candidates.

This chapter will help you to understand:

- the National Occupational Standards for Children's Care, Learning and Development and how to use them effectively
- the contribution of the National Occupational Standards to the Children's Workforce Development Strategy
- the importance of the Principles and Values.

Check it out

Throughout this chapter, references will be made to specific pieces of legislation, so you will find it useful to obtain copies of and make yourself familiar with the following documents, all of which are available from the Department for Education and Skills (DfES) at www.dfes.gov.uk; www.scotland.gov.uk

- The Green Paper – Every Child Matters
- The Children's Workforce Strategy
- The Lead Professional Good Practice Guidance
- The Common Core of Skills and Knowledge
- The National Strategy for Improving Adult Literacy and Numeracy

The National Occupational Standards for Children's Care, Learning and Development and how to use them effectively

The introduction of the new National Occupational Standards (NOS) in Children's Care, Learning and Development (CCLD) in October 2005 was generally well received, with the majority of practitioners feeling that a redevelopment of the award was necessary. Consultation within the occupational field indicated that the sector needed NOS that were easy to follow, jargon free and easily accessible. Redevelopment of the NOS acknowledged that practitioners often carry out a variety of job roles, working within a range of settings with a diverse cross-section of families. The decision to increase the age range from 0–8 years to 0–16 years allowed the award to be accessible to more practitioners and the wider selection of optional units provided support for practitioners from many settings. Practitioners from diverse backgrounds and settings could therefore consider training towards this award, rather than alternative qualifications that might not have fully fitted their individual requirements. For example, practitioners working with children in after-school clubs or youth clubs may have traditionally opted for the Playwork NVQ, which was a qualification sufficient for that job role. However, it left them with little scope to move into other areas of childcare, and meant that should they wish to work with younger children, they would have to retrain. The CCLD NOS have addressed this issue, and the range of optional units available has enabled practitioners across the field to find it accessible and achievable, while also being flexible enough to see them through their current and prospective job roles.

What are the National Occupational Standards?

The NOS define the outcomes that we expect candidates to reach. They show what skills, knowledge and understanding are needed for employment within the sector, and guide candidates towards the expected achievement, while also helping the assessor to make judgements of competence. It is essential that you understand that the NOS are not specific training courses, but that they clearly demonstrate the criteria to be achieved and the aspects of competence required, setting a benchmark for best practice, as well as indicating acceptable levels of service. The NOS also ensure that both the assessor and the candidate are clear about the scope and depth of competence and the knowledge requirements that the candidate needs to demonstrate.

The NOS may also be used in ways other than within training and qualifications. For instance, a manager of a private day nursery might use the NOS as a tool when writing job descriptions for her employees. She could use them to specify best practice requirements and performance indicators, such as for target setting and structure of supervision. After-school clubs might use the NOS for employee development, marketing or business planning and Sure Start centres could use them for appraisals or workforce management. However they are used, the NOS have been designed to provide a basis for those who work with children and young people in a variety of settings.

Over to you!
Performance Criteria

Look at *Unit 201 Contribute to positive relationships* within the CCLD Level 2 NOS. Find *Element 201.1 Interact with and respond to children.*

1 Find the box containing the Performance Criteria.
2 Read the list of criteria and consider how they set a benchmark for best practice.
3 Think about how the criteria demonstrate acceptable levels of service.

The structure of the NOS

The NOS for CCLD are broken down into **units**. The units are individually numbered and are either optional or mandatory. Table 1 summarises the structure of the NOS.

Table 1   The structure of the NOS

Level	Total units	Mandatory	Optional	Optional groups
Level 2	7	6	1	N/A
Level 3	9	5	4	2 units from group 1 2 units from group 1 or 2
Level 4	9	4	5	N/A

Unit

Describes a particular function within a job and breaks it down to list the specific activities or duties this comprises. Indicates the functions that the candidate is required to carry out in the workplace, forming the building blocks that make up the qualification

Check it out

You can find out more about the transitional playwork modules at www.playwork.org.uk

Element

Describes one distinct aspect of the function depicted by the unit. Identifies one particular aspect of the work that the candidate must be able to do

The optional unit choices at all levels will depend upon a candidate's job roles and future career goals. We will look at this in more detail later in the chapter (see pages 22–23).

There are also two transitional modules that will enable candidates to move between the playwork and childcare sectors without having to gain additional full qualifications. These modules enable Level 3 qualified practitioners to gain a qualification in playwork following 60 hours of guided learning.

At the beginning of each unit, you will find a page that provides both the candidate and yourself with information about the content of that particular unit. It acts as a summary for the unit, identifying what the unit is about and who it is for. This information is particularly useful for candidates when choosing their optional units, so you should encourage them to read this information.

Following on from this information is *Key Words and Concepts*. This section explains and defines key words used within the unit, as they may be used in a particular way. Many candidates miss out this important information, going directly to the main *Performance Criteria*. However, this section can be extremely useful in understanding the main point of the unit before the candidate begins.

Each unit is divided into **elements**. The elements demonstrate particular aspects of that unit. Candidates must show competence in all elements in order to complete the qualification. The number of elements within each unit will vary.

Over to you!
Units

Look at your NOS for CCLD Level 3. What are the particular functions of the following units?

303 _____

_____

305 _____

_____

311 _____

_____

326 _____

_____

Over to you!
Elements

Look at your NOS for Level 2. Find *Unit 203 Support children's development*. This unit has four elements. Write the names of these elements in the spaces below.

203.1 _____

_____

203.2 _____

_____

203.3 _____

_____

203.4 _____

_____

Elements are broken down further into **Performance Criteria** (PCs). This list of PCs identifies several criteria that the candidate must fulfil in order to demonstrate competence.

Performance Criteria

Describe one distinct aspect of the function depicted by the unit. Identify a particular aspect of the work that the candidate must be able to do

Over to you!
Performance Criteria 2

Find *Unit 301 Develop and promote positive relationships* within the Level 3 NOS. Make a note of the PCs within *Element 301.2 Communicate with children.*

1 _____
_____
2 _____
_____
3 _____
_____
4 _____
_____
5 _____
_____

At the end of each unit, the NOS provide a list of **Knowledge Specifications**. These indicators identify the knowledge and understanding that is required to carry out competent practice in the performance described in the unit.

Knowledge Specification

Describes what is necessary for the candidate to know and understand in order to be competent in a variety of work contexts and at different times. This forms the foundation for each unit. Without this knowledge the candidate cannot prove competence

Over to you!
Knowledge Specifications

Look at the Knowledge Specifications for *Unit 205 Prepare and maintain environments to meet children's needs*. Make a note of the following Knowledge Specifications.

K2D60 _____

_____

K2D69 _____

_____

K2H78 _____

_____

The diagram below shows how the numbering for the Knowledge Specifications has been devised.

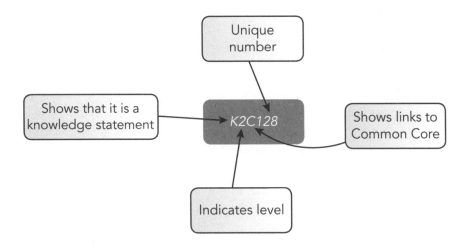

At this point you should look through both sets of NOS, identifying the units, elements, performance criteria and knowledge specifications. Familiarise yourself with the layout of the NOS, and the language used. They may seem confusing at first, but the more you work with them, the more they will become useable.

How have the National Occupational Standards for CCLD changed?

Title change

Those of you familiar with the NOS for EYCE will notice some changes immediately, though some are more subtle than others. The first and most dominant change has been the name of the NOS. As the term *early years* does not have the same meaning in each of the four home countries of the UK – England, Northern Ireland, Scotland and Wales – it was felt that the previous name *Early Years Care and Education* could mislead practitioners. It was noted that many practitioners, such as childminders and those who worked with children with special or additional needs, felt that although the EYCE NOS met their training needs, the age range was a barrier, as they often worked with children over the age of eight years. Extended school provision has also meant that more and more practitioners are working in settings that cater for children over the 0–8 age range and multi-disciplinary approaches to working require knowledge of an extended age range.

Removal of italics

Within the previous standards, you may have noticed that some of the Performance Criteria were presented in *italics*. This indicated to the assessor and candidate that those particular Performance Criteria 'might not be covered when your assessor is observing you, and you may have to produce other types of evidence to cover these'. It was felt that this was too prescriptive and needed to be addressed if the revised standards were to be assessed holistically. The removal of the *italics* now enables assessors to observe in a more holistic way, making direct observation the focus of the award and preventing the need for unnecessary additional evidence to be produced by the candidate. Where assessors are not able to observe particular Performance Criteria, they can now observe product evidence instead.

Age range

The reasons for the changes to the name of the award have impacted on the age range of the specifications and the new NOS now cover the age range 0–16. Throughout the NOS, you will find that the context, rather than the age of the child, is highlighted, stressing the importance of candidates working within an individual child's developmental capacity, rather than chronological age bands.

Over to you!
Removal of italics

Take a look at Unit C1.1 within the EYCE Level 2 NOS. You will see that Performance Criteria 5 to 9 are in *italics*. Look at each of these PCs and consider how you might assess them if they were written into the new CCLD NOS.

Candidates are required to have a sound knowledge and understanding of the 0–16 age range, regardless of which age group they actually work with. This knowledge and understanding allows candidates to be flexible, offering transferable skills, should they wish to work with a different age range in the future.

The extended age range provides greater flexibility within the childcare workforce, and allows practitioners to develop wider career goals.

Check it out

A good example of reference to developmental milestones rather than age can be found in Unit 203, Element 2, in particular Performance Criteria 3, which states:
'Support children's positive behaviour, according to the procedures of the setting, giving praise and encouragement as appropriate according to the child's age, needs and abilities.'

Case study Aspirations Training

Tracy Jarratt, an NVQ assessor at Aspirations Training in Birmingham, has seen how the extended age range has offered her candidates greater choice and flexibility in their training. She states:

'Having the age range up to 16 years means that my candidates now have more choice about the type of setting where they work and practise. Previously, some candidates wanted to work within Key Stage 2, but the old NOS were too restrictive and didn't lend themselves to being assessed within this older age group. Many of my candidates now try a variety of settings, including after-school clubs, youth clubs and holiday play schemes, as part of their placements, offering them more real work experience from which to draw when they decide how to progress their career. Obviously some candidates come to me with a clear picture of their career path and may stick with the younger children in their work practice, but the new NOS give them the opportunity to learn about a child's whole development, and therefore increase their career opportunities for the future. The wide range of optional units also enables the candidates to tailor their learning to their own needs and future goals.'

Language and terminology

You may also have noticed that the CCLD NOS are simpler in their language and terminology than the EYCE NOS. Feedback from the consultation process showed that NOS that were clear, easy to read and accessible were very important to practitioners.

Over to you!

Key changes

Compare the following two units from the EYCE and CCLD NOS:

- *EYCE Level 2 Unit E2.3 Carry out emergency procedures*
- *CCLD Level 2 Unit 202.2 Follow procedures for accidents, emergencies and illness*

Identify the key changes that have been made, considering the language and terminology used, and the differences in the criteria.

Imported units

The CCLD NOS consist of 87 units of competence, 22 of which have been imported from other awards – *Playwork, Health and Social Care, Management and Leadership, Teaching Assistants*, and *Learning and Development*. Again, this has widened the scope for candidates, offering them flexible opportunities and career routes.

Check it out

You can obtain a copy of the CCLD assessment strategy at www.cwdcouncil.org.uk

Should a candidate have already completed and imported units, they will not be required to repeat them; they should be fully accredited through a direct transfer via your awarding body. The assessment strategy for CCLD will apply to all the imported units and assessment of these units should be carried out by occupationally competent assessors.

You should now have an understanding of how the CCLD NOS are designed and be able to find your way around them. It is worth taking the time to make yourself familiar with the layout and terminology. You may find it useful to obtain your own copy, in which you can make notes and prompts to help you navigate yourself around them.

The contribution of the National Occupational Standards to the Children's Workforce Development Strategy

'A strategy to build a world-class workforce for children and young people'

In the summer of 2005, the government consulted on its proposed Children's Workforce Strategy, describing a 'vision for a world-class children's workforce'.

Check it out

You can download a copy of the Children's Workforce Strategy at www.dfes.gov.uk; www.scotland.gov.uk

In her foreword within the strategy, Margaret Hodge, MP MBE, describes the strategy as '… our plans to create a world-class workforce which is increasingly competent and confident to make a difference to the lives of those they support. Such a workforce will be one that people aspire to join and are loath to leave.'

With a vision to improve outcomes, and build multi-disciplinary teams, the strategy illustrates the government's 'key strategic challenges' across children's services, namely to:

1 recruit more people into the children's workforce
2 develop and retain more people within the children's workforce

3 strengthen inter-agency and multi-disciplinary workforce and workforce remodelling

4 promote stronger leadership, management and supervision.

The strategy looks at how to meet these challenges and improve the skills and knowledge of those working with children and young people. Each of these key challenges will determine how your role as an assessor is developed, as well as the knowledge and skills that you will be required to pass on to your candidates.

1 Recruit more people into the children's workforce

Recruitment of competent, confident practitioners is vital to the success of the Children's Workforce Development Strategy. On a national level, you may have seen advertising campaigns, promoting careers in teaching, childcare, social work, social care, nursing and midwifery. Although these have been successful, the strategy states that regional and local recruitment campaigns are more effective.

To support this challenge, the government established new Sector Skills Council arrangements for the children's workforce and developed the Children's Workforce Development Council (CWDC). Established in April 2005, the CWDC is a member of the federated Sector Skills Council for Social Care, Children and Young People (Skills for Care and Development SSC). Developed to build a workforce for children, young people and families, it supports 'the whole workforce to put the child, young person and family at the heart of service design and delivery'.

Playing a central role in delivering the workforce reform, its six strategic objectives have been developed to support the workforce strategy in building a world-class workforce, with the first objective focusing on improving 'the recruitment, retention and development of appropriately skilled staff to the wider children, young people and families workforce '.

The strategy recommends that local workforce strategies be developed as an integral part of the Children and Young People's Plan, and the CWDC supports the development and implementation of these local strategies.

> **Check it out**
>
> Find out more about the work of the Children's Workforce Development Council at www.cwdcouncil.org.uk

Over to you!
Overcoming barriers

Think about some of the barriers that candidates may come across when trying to enter the childcare workforce. What are the main factors that influence a person to take an offer of employment? Do you feel that these barriers and factors affect candidates while training? As an assessor, what could you do to overcome these factors/barriers for your candidates?

The under-representation of men in the sector

Men make up a small minority of childcare workers, under-represented within both employment and training. Research figures show that only 2 to 3 per cent of the childcare workforce are male. Within playwork, the figures are slightly higher, with men making up almost 10 per cent of the workforce.

Over to you!
Under-representation of men

Imagine that you are giving a recruitment presentation to a secondary school in your area. Many of the young men in the school have commented that childcare training is for girls. Describe how you would present the sector to the young people in the school, giving your case for increasing the participation of men.

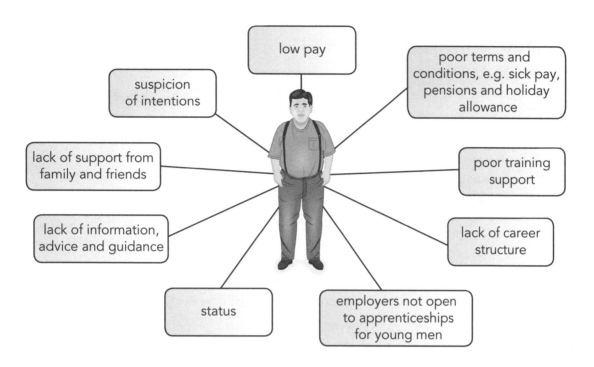

What barriers do men face in employment within the childcare sector and what can you do to overcome these barriers?

It is important to note that these barriers also apply to other members of the workforce, not just to men.

Over to you!
Recruiting more men

List five things that you could do within your centre to actively recruit more men onto the CCLD S/NVQ.

1 _____

_____

2 _____

_____

3 _____

_____

4 _____

_____

5 _____

_____

Case study   Men into Childcare Project

Bradford Early Years and Childcare Service has been working with other local authorities in the West Yorkshire region to develop the National Men into Childcare Pilot Project. The activities focused on Male Taster Sessions and Male Focus Groups.

'We recently held a free Male Taster Session at a central venue in Bradford, to help to encourage men to take up a career working with children and young people. Ten men interested in working with children and young people attended the session and were given advice and information on the training and qualifications needed to work with children and young people and the range of jobs within the sector. The men were interested in many different areas of work with children and young people, including Playwork, Education, Youth Offending Work, Connexions and Children's Residential Homes.

The session was a success, with seven men signed up to receive further information and guidance. We will be closely monitoring the progression of the attendees. To date:

- two of the men signed up to attend the Playwork Basics Introductory training course
- three men have expressed an interest in shadowing an experienced male playwork practitioner
- the Bradford Early Years and Childcare Service Outreach and Mentoring Worker is mentoring five of the men from the session.

We also recently organised a Male Focus Group Session. This was attended by men who are working or volunteering in an early years, childcare or playwork setting in the Bradford District. This focus group discussed topics such as the effectiveness of the current marketing and publicity that Bradford Early Years and Childcare Service uses, what attracts men to work with children, and the perceived barriers that deter men from considering childcare as a career.

The feedback gained from the focus group is being used to prepare a promotional leaflet to assist us in recruiting more men into the sector.

As a result of this session, we have developed a network of men working with children and young people to offer ongoing mentoring and job shadowing services to new male recruits.'

Under-representation of minority groups

Minority group

A secondary group whose members have significantly less control or power over their lives than members of a dominant or majority group.

Minority groups are under-represented within the childcare employment sector. Many childcare settings acknowledge the diverse experience and richness that can be brought into the setting by practitioners from alternative cultural, religious or community groups; however, these groups are still very much in the minority. When thinking in terms of diversity and minority groups, it is essential to remember that this encompasses a variety of communities including travellers, asylum seekers and refugees, and that combating educational and social exclusion is very important. Employing practitioners from diverse cultural, religious and community backgrounds will support the emotional development of children from the same group, as well as enriching the experiences of children from alternative groups. Childcare settings are developing their awareness of the diverse cultures and customs that are prevalent within society, and encouraging children to learn about these within the setting. Employing practitioners from these groups can bring real-life experience to the children. It is important that employers are sensitive to the individual needs of the practitioner, from whatever group.

One way to address these issues is to be proactive in the recruitment of minority groups into training. We discussed many ways of doing this for men, and these strategies can also be used for minority groups. By being sensitive and open to the diverse needs of people from these groups, you can support them in overcoming barriers to learning and encourage them to work towards their training and career goals, thus bringing depth and richness into the sector. You will need to think of creative, innovative ways of making training accessible and attractive, while understanding the experiences, perceptions and attitudes of potential candidates.

You should take into account the early educational experiences of the candidates and address any underlying issues these may have caused. Young people who have experienced discrimination in their early education may feel that further training will bring the same prejudice. Once educational attainment has been affected by racism or discrimination, many people find it difficult to return to education and, ultimately, find difficulties in gaining employment. Racism, discrimination, myths, stereotyping and ignorance are all factors that will influence education and training opportunities.

Case study Witchford Village College

'Witchford Village College, a rural secondary college, has children from gypsy and fairground backgrounds. The social inclusion of these pupils is a key feature of the college. Profiles of each child's progress, attainment and college engagement are drawn up and regularly maintained. Early interventions on issues of attendance, parental support and pupil behaviour keep the confidence of the parents in the college's efforts to integrate their children. Continued attendance at the college is confirmed by the principal and governors' clearly stated written commitment to gypsy traveller pupils.'

Aiming High; Raising the Achievement of Gypsy Traveller Pupils, DFES, July 2003

Over to you!
Promoting childcare training

Think about how your centre/college/region promotes childcare training and employment. Are there any particular campaigns that have been successful, or any promotional incentives that you feel have recruited more people into the children's workforce? What would you do to promote childcare training in your area, particularly within under-represented groups?

2 Develop and retain more people within the children's workforce

Retaining professional and committed practitioners within childcare is not always easy, with many stating that low pay and poor terms and conditions are the main reasons for their leaving the sector. The strategy recognises the importance of developing the skills of practitioners and building rewarding careers to develop and maintain the workforce. It states:

> '… we are taking national action to establish better career pathways founded on increased commonality of skills and knowledge and driven by a new national infrastructure to support workforce development.'

The proposed action within the Green Paper *Every Child Matters* to develop a set of common, basic skills and knowledge was strongly supported and during 2004 the DfES presented a Common Core of Skills and Knowledge for the Children's Workforce. This set out six areas of expertise, describing the required basic levels of knowledge and skills to which all practitioners should be working.

1 Effective communication and engagement with children, young people, their families and carers
2 Child and young person development
3 Safeguarding and promoting welfare of the child
4 Supporting transitions
5 Multi-agency working
6 Sharing information

This common set of skills, knowledge and competence will support the development of integrated services, providing practitioners, support staff and professionals with a 'common

Check it out

Obtain your copy of the *Common Core of Skills* at www.dfes.gov.uk/commoncore; www.scotland.gov.uk

language', thus reducing some of the barriers we looked at earlier. Having a common framework to consider provides employers with a tool for staff training and development and allows practitioners to develop their skills and knowledge and improve job satisfaction.

Over to you!
The Common Core

It is your role as an assessor to inform your candidates of initiatives such as the Common Core and to support them in understanding how such initiatives impact on their training and future employment. Look through the Common Core and identify how you could introduce this to your candidates and ensure that they are aware of the implications of it. How do you feel the Common Core fits into the CCLD S/NVQ?

The following table shows all the mandatory units of both the Level 2 and Level 3 CCLD S/NVQs and gives examples of how the Common Core fits into each unit. Take a look at the Knowledge Specifications within each unit and notice how they relate strongly to the skills identified in the Common Core.

Table 2 Links between CCLD and the Common Core

Unit	Title	Links to Common Core
201	Contribute to positive relationships	**1** Effective communication and engagement with children, young people, their families and carers • Listening and building empathy • Consultation and negotiation • How communication works • Importance of respect • Sources of support
202	Help to keep children safe	**3** Safeguarding and promoting welfare of the child • Relate, recognise and take considered action • Communication, recording and reporting • Legal and procedural frameworks • Wider context of services • Self-knowledge
203	Support children's development	**2** Child and young person development • Observation and judgement • Understand context • Empathy and understanding • Understand how babies, children and young people develop
204	Use support systems to develop own practice in CCLD	**5** Multi-agency working • Communication and teamwork • Assertiveness • Your role and remit • Procedures and working methods • Know how to make queries • The law, policies and procedures
205	Prepare and maintain environments to meet children's needs	**4** Supporting transitions • Provide support • How children and young people respond to change • When and how to intervene
206	Support children's play and learning	**2** Child and young person development • Observation and judgement • Understand context • Empathy and understanding • Know how to reflect and improve • Be clear about your own job role • Understand how babies, children and young people develop

Unit	Title	Links to Common Core
301	Develop and promote positive relationships	**1** Effective communication and engagement with children, young people, their families and carers • Listening and building empathy • Consultation and negotiation • How communication works • Importance of respect • Sources of support
302	Develop and maintain a healthy, safe and secure environment for children	**3** Safeguarding and promoting welfare of the child • Relate, recognise and take considered action • Communication, recording and reporting • Legal and procedural frameworks • Wider context of services • Self-knowledge
303	Promote children's development	**2** Child and young person development • Observation and judgement • Understand context • Empathy and understanding • Know how to reflect and improve • Be clear about your own job role • Understand how babies, children and young people develop
304	Reflect on and develop practice	**5** Multi-agency working • Communication and teamwork • Assertiveness • Your role and remit • Procedures and working methods • Know how to make queries • The law, policies and procedures • Know how to reflect and improve
305	Protect and promote children's rights	**6** Sharing information • Information handling • Clear communication • Engagement • Role and responsibilities • Importance of information sharing • Awareness of complexities • Awareness of laws and legislation • Confidentiality and ethics

Previously within this chapter, when looking at the Knowledge Specifications within the NOS, you looked at how the numbering for the Knowledge Specifications had been devised (see page 7). The diagram showed that the middle letter identified the grouping of the Knowledge Specifications. This links directly to the Common Core of Skills and Knowledge in the following way.

Table 3 Referencing links to the Common Core

Letter	Link to Common Core of Skills and Knowledge
C	Effective communication and engagement with children, young people, their families and carers
D	Child and young person development
H	Health and safety
M	Multi-agency working and sharing information
P	Occupational practice
S	Safeguarding children and promoting the welfare of the child
T	Supporting transitions

Developing career pathways

The introduction of the CCLD S/NVQ has supported the importance of improving skills and career pathways as detailed within the Green Paper *Every Child Matters*. With a range of optional units and imported units from other sectors, candidates have never had so much freedom to build qualifications that support and guide their individual career paths. Candidates working at Level 2 are generally working as assistants or under direct supervision. At Level 3, the qualifications range available is much broader, and requires much thought. Candidates working at Level 3 will generally

have more responsibility and will be able to work unsupervised.
Examples of possible job roles at each level are shown in the
table below.

Table 4 Possible job roles at Levels 2 and 3

Level 2	Level 3
Nursery assistant	Nursery nurse
Crèche worker	Officer in charge
Family support assistant	Family worker
Special needs assistant	Supporting health care professionals
Childminder	Childminder
Playscheme assistant	Playscheme leader

Over to you!
Which units?

Read the following scenarios and consider which optional units you would recommend for each candidate.

1 A Level 2 female candidate has been offered employment within a holiday playscheme. It is for the summer only, after which she hopes to work within a private day nursery.
2 A Level 3 male candidate is employed within a school as a special educational needs support worker. He wants to keep his options open and is considering moving into working with 14–16-year-olds with special needs.
3 A Level 3 female candidate is hoping to continue on to higher education and qualify as a social worker, specialising in working with children and families.

The lead professional

The introduction of Children's Centres and the emphasis on improving integrated working across services has opened the doors to improved practice and new role boundaries. To ensure that these joined-up childcare and family service approaches are coherent and well managed, the government stated:

'Our vision is that such integrated support can be most effectively delivered through one practitioner acting in a "lead role" – a lead professional.'

The role of the lead professional is to act as a single point of contact who children, young people and families can trust and whom is able to support them in making choices and moving through the system. This professional will ensure that children and families have access to support and guidance when needed and that the support offered is well planned, regularly reviewed and effectively delivered. The introduction of this role should reduce overlap and inconsistency from other practitioners, preventing families from being given conflicting advice. The guidance on this role states that:

'Lead professionals need the confidence and competence to:

- develop a successful and productive relationship with the child and family, and communicate without jargon
- support the child and/or family in implementing a range of strategies to enable them to achieve their potential
- convene meetings and discussions with different practitioners
- use the Common Assessment Framework and develop support plans based on the outcomes
- co-ordinate the delivery of effective early intervention work and ongoing support
- work in partnership with other practitioners to deliver the support plan
- communicate effectively to ensure that all support is fully co-ordinated.'

The Early Years Professional

Within the consultation of the children's workforce, the need for the development of the role for the Early Years Professional (EYP) was also identified. It is the government's aim to have

Check it out

Find out more about the Common Assessment Framework at www.everychildmatters. gov.uk/deliveringservices/ caf; www.scotland.gov.uk

EYPs in all Children's Centres that offer early years provision by 2010 and in every full day-care setting by 2015. The EYP role is key to the delivery of governmental targets and will raise the quality of early years provision by improving and leading practice, developing a supportive mentor role and promoting positive outcomes for children. The qualification for this role is equivalent in level to qualified teacher status and therefore candidates will undergo rigorous and in-depth training. There are a range of entry routes onto the EYP training.

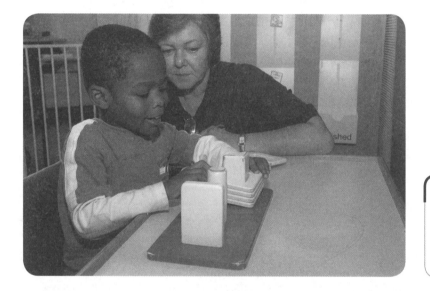

Check it out

Find out more about Early Years Professional status at www.cwdcouncil.org.uk

Over to you!
Continuous professional development

An experienced and fully qualified practitioner approaches you for advice on her professional development. She has recently been promoted to the lead professional role at the family centre where she works. She wants to work towards three units of the CCLD S/NVQ as part of her continuous professional development and to update her skills. Which three units would you recommend she work towards?

1 _____

_____

2 _____

_____

3 _____

_____

Retention and development of candidates

It is important that your candidates are introduced to these initiatives and understand the roles and responsibilities of the lead professional. Some of them might even become lead professionals within their own settings. Candidates will require an understanding of the role, recognising how it fits into integrated services and how their position plays a part in this. You could offer this information during a discussion on practitioner roles, examining the various employment routes and careers within the sector. Think about ways you could disseminate information on the lead professional and EYP roles to your candidates. Table 5 shows how delivery of individual Level 3 mandatory units can provide an opportunity to discuss the skills and knowledge required within this initiative.

Training centres need to be proactive and innovative in their strategies to support retention and development of their candidates.

Case study Cannock Chase Technical College

Cannock Chase Technical College in Staffordshire uses a variety of approaches to promote, develop and retain candidates on their work-based learning routes.

'We try to offer clear information from the outset to ensure that candidates are fully informed of their commitment and responsibility to the courses they are enrolling on. We find that taster days are very popular, giving candidates the opportunity to be hands-on and get a feel for the course before deciding whether it's for them. We also provide open days and evenings, encouraging potential candidates to take a look around our facilities and chat with the assessors and tutors on the course. Careers events through Connexions and school careers evenings are successful in attracting young people and links with the local job centre enable us to target mature candidates as well. We have also offered financial incentives on completion, giving candidates something to aim for.'

Table 5 Links to lead professional role

Skills and knowledge required within lead professional	Possible discussion topics	Unit
Develop a successful and productive relationship with the child and family, and communicate without jargon	Legislation	301
	Confidentiality	301
	Communication	301
	Discrimination	305
	Reflective practice	304
Support the child and/or family in implementing a range of strategies to enable them to achieve their potential	Anti-discriminatory practice	301
	Behaviour management	301
	Assessment strategies	303
	Child development	303
	Importance of play	303
	Reflective practice	304
Convene meetings and discussions with different practitioners	Communication	301
	Health and safety law	302
	Verbal and non-verbal communication	301
	Reflective practice	304
Use the Common Assessment Framework and develop support plans based on the outcomes	Assessment strategies	303
	Inclusion	305
	Building relationships	301
	Reflective practice	304
Co-ordinate the delivery of effective early intervention work and ongoing support	Making referrals	303
	Assessment strategies	303
	Reflective practice	304
Work in partnership with other practitioners to deliver the support plan	Building relationships	301
	Inclusion	305
	Communication	301
	Reflective practice	304
Communicate effectively to ensure that all support is fully co-ordinated	Communication	301
	Child protection	305
	Reflective practice	304

3 Strengthen inter-agency and multi-disciplinary workforce and workforce remodelling

The diverse, multi-cultural society in which we live dictates a multi-disciplinary workforce. The joining together of sectors, departments and professionals ensures that the work carried out is effective, developed and structured. Multi-agency working can be carried out in a variety of ways and there are no hard and fast rules as to how this should be done.

As training practitioners, your candidates will have differing levels of experience of multi-agency working. Many of your candidates will be in direct contact with children and families and, as such, need to be aware of how to work effectively with other agencies.

Inter-agency working

A range of agencies working together to achieve more outcomes than if working in isolation

The idea of inter-agency working can be introduced to your candidates at the beginning of their training, and the approach will run through the length of their S/NVQ.

Sure Start Children's Centres are ideal examples of multi-agency approaches to delivery. Many centres offer parents access to a range of professionals that may include:

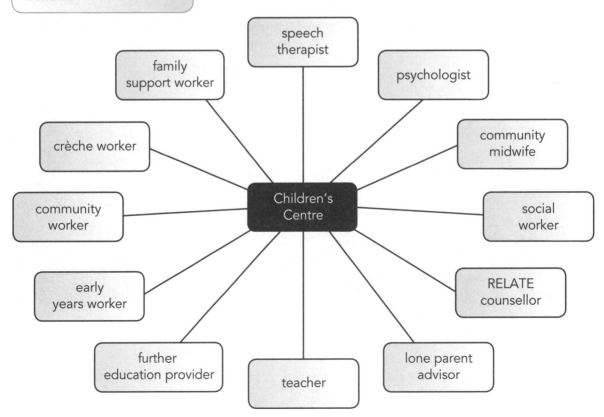

This range of professionals will support children and families within a variety of contexts, such as behaviour management, smoking cessation and breast-feeding support. The practitioners all need to work coherently to ensure that the child and family receive the most effective support for their needs. This need for a coherent service demonstrates the requirement for the lead professional role, as discussed earlier. This lead professional becomes the main point of contact for parents and families, ensuring the best possible outcome for them. Your candidates need to understand and learn about the importance of inter-agency working to enable them to access a range of job roles in a variety of childcare settings.

To develop this inter-agency approach further, the DfES has produced a series of toolkits:

- *Toolkit for managers of multi-agency panels*
- *Toolkit for managers of multi-agency teams*
- *Toolkit for managers of integrated services*
- *Toolkit for practitioners*

These web-based toolkits aim to support managers and practitioners and are structured around the three service delivery models:

1 multi-agency panel
2 multi-agency team
3 integrated service.

The toolkits provide examples of good practice and it is anticipated that, as they develop, they will provide a platform for sharing good practice. The toolkits focus on a number of issues, including effective multi-agency working and common language, and work through some of the challenges faced by this inter-agency approach.

Integrated working means that new candidates require the skills to allow them to work effectively and strategically at different levels. They need to understand the diverse sector in which they are planning to work, and how their roles will require them to work alongside a variety of practitioners.

> ### Check it out
> Find out more about multi-disciplinary working at www.connexions.gov.uk

> ### Check it out
> Try the toolkits out for yourself at www.ecm.gov.uk/multiagencyworking/practitionerstoolkit

Over to you!
Skills and knowledge

You have a Level 3 candidate who is employed full-time as a Sure Start Family Worker. List three important skills or knowledge areas the candidate requires that are relevant to her post and consider how you might support her in the development of these skills during her CCLD training.

1 _____

_____

_____

_____

2 _____

_____

_____

_____

3 _____

_____

_____

_____

_____

4 Promote stronger leadership, management and supervision

'Effective leadership nationally and locally will be essential to drive through workforce reform... To achieve this we need action both to support existing leaders and to develop the leaders of the future.'
Children's workforce strategy, DfES, 2005

It is important to remember that the candidates of today may be the leaders of tomorrow and that, as an assessor, you will have a guiding hand in realising their full potential. Candidates should be provided with information on further and higher education, have the opportunity to explore alternative training routes, and have the confidence to strive for the career they deserve.

The development of a national programme to address the needs of leaders within the sector – the National Professional Qualification in Integrated Centre Leadership (NPQICL) – will fully support this agenda. NPQICL will be recognised as a qualification in working in multi-agency and multi-disciplinary environments across education, health and social services. Offering a choice of study or research routes, participants can either work through a range of modules, or undertake research focusing on their own leadership role.

Your candidates may want to progress to CCLD Level 4, which is for practitioners working in management roles. This award is not as widely available as Levels 2 and 3, but information on this route should be made available to candidates who want to further their career and learning. It is also essential that candidates are fully informed of the commitment required for this level of training, as well as the prior experience required.

The importance of the Principles and Values

When working with and supporting people within the childcare sector, there are certain basic principles and values that affect everything you believe and guide everything you do. These principles and values thread through every area of practice and impact on the work of your candidates and the families and children they have contact with. There are three Principles and nine Values, which underpin the whole set of NOS, including the imported units.

Principles

1 The welfare of the child is paramount.
2 Practitioners contribute to children's care, learning and development and this is reflected in every aspect of practice and service provision.
3 Practitioners work with parents and families, who are partners in the care, learning and development of their children and the child's first and most enduring educators.

Values

1 The needs, rights and views of the child are at the centre of all practice and provision.
2 Individuality, difference and diversity are valued and celebrated.

> ### Check it out
>
> Find out more about this qualification at www.ncsl.org.uk

3 Equality of opportunity and anti-discriminatory practice are actively promoted.

4 Children's health and well-being are actively promoted.

5 Children's personal and physical safety is safeguarded, while allowing for risk and challenge as appropriate to the capabilities of the child.

6 Self-esteem, resilience and a positive self-image are recognised as essential to a child's development.

7 Confidentiality and agreements about confidential information are respected as appropriate unless a child's protection and well-being are at stake.

8 Professional knowledge, skills and values are shared appropriately in order to enrich the experience of children more widely.

9 Best practice requires reflection and a continuous search for improvement.

Competency
Having the necessary skill or knowledge to do something successfully.

These Principles and Values form the foundations of the S/NVQ, therefore, your candidates require a full understanding of how the Principles and Values impact on their practice so they can correctly interpret and understand the NOS. During your assessment of your candidates you will be looking for evidence of **competency**. Before you can assess your candidates as competent, you must ensure that they have demonstrated that they work within the framework of the Principles and Values.

The introduction to the CCLD NOS 2005 states:

'The awarding bodies are required to ensure that assessors provide a statement against each unit to testify that candidates have demonstrated the application of such principles and values.'

This statement will differ depending on the awarding body your assessment centre is using however, it may read something like this:

I ___Sarah Jones___ (name of assessor) **confirm that this candidate** _Mary Brown_ (name of candidate)

has achieved all the requirements of this unit, including working within the context of the

Principles and Values of the Children's Care, Learning & Development sector.

Assessment was conducted under the specified conditions and context, and is valid, authentic,

reliable, current and sufficient.

Signed assessor ___*Sarah Jones*_____   Date ___31/07/07_____

Signed candidate ___Mary Brown_____   Date ___31/07/07_____

Over to you!
The Principles and Values

Imagine that you are assessing a candidate carrying out a music and movement session with the children in his care. The candidate has a variety of music, including music from a range of cultural groups. He is encouraging the children to move their bodies to the music, and is joining in with them. How might this assessment demonstrate to you the candidate's ability to work within the contexts of the Principles and Values?

_____

_____

_____

_____

_____

_____

_____

_____

Check your understanding

As you have reached the end of this chapter, you may find it useful to consolidate all that you have learnt by answering the following questions. You will find suggested answers in the back of the book on page 169.

1 What do the National Occupational Standards define?
2 How many units make up a Level 3 qualification and how are they broken into mandatory and optional units?
3 What is the role of transitional modules?
4 What is an element?
5 Identify three ways in which the CCLD NOS are different from the EYCE NOS.
6 What is the role of the Children's Workforce Development Council?
7 Name two under-represented groups within the childcare sector.
8 What is the Common Core of Skills?
9 Identify appropriate job roles at Levels 2 and 3.
10 What are the three Principles of the childcare sector?

Chapter 2

Supporting candidates

Introduction

Having worked through Chapter 1, you should now be familiar with the National Occupational Standards (NOS) for Children's Care, Learning and Development (CCLD) and their context within the day-to-day lives of people working with children. Before you can begin to assess your candidates towards these standards, you must first understand the importance of good professional relationships and how these will support your work with your candidates. The type of relationship you have with your candidates will most certainly make a huge difference to the way they learn and develop throughout their training and will also affect your ability to work with them in an appropriate manner. This chapter looks at how to build the most effective relationships with candidates, depending upon their individual needs, abilities and learning styles. You will learn how to work with your candidates and provide training that is individual to them and develops each of them as a whole person.

This chapter will help you to understand:
- the importance of building effective relationships with candidates
- how to support candidates with additional needs
- how to ensure differentiation between candidates.

The importance of building effective relationships with candidates

Building relationships with candidates is a key element in the development of learning and education. The quality of the relationship formed between you and your candidates will have a lasting impact on their learning and is central to the development of opportunities for them to develop, grow and change. The foundations of any relationship are trust, respect and honesty, and these must come from both parties in order to build a mutual relationship.

A successful relationship is based on respect, the ability to listen to each other and the ability to respond in an appropriate manner. Having an open and honest association, in which both candidates and yourself can speak out and talk about your feelings, is central to building a sound professional relationship. It is essential that you offer a climate in which candidates can learn with and from each other successfully. This climate, or learning environment, should offer reassurance that confidentiality will be maintained at all times.

Confidentiality

Throughout the Children's Care, Learning and Development (CCLD) S/NVQ, you will be promoting the importance of **confidentiality** to your candidates. You will be explaining their role in maintaining confidential information about children and how this information should be stored. Your candidates will need to demonstrate their knowledge of and commitment to legal requirements as to the protection of children and the maintenance of their records, such as the Data Protection Act 1998.

All of these principles and practices should also apply to the way in which you maintain the confidentiality of your candidates. From time to time your candidates may disclose information to you which is personal to them, and this should remain confidential. This information may be relevant to you in order for you to understand their individual needs, but they may not want others to have this information. Your candidate will be demonstrating a great deal of trust when disclosing information to you and it is therefore essential that you do not break this trust by breaching confidentiality. If the trust between yourself and the candidate breaks down, so will the relationship. Any information given to you by a candidate should only be shared with others with the candidate's consent. For example, it may be necessary to share information with other assessors, tutors or verifiers, but this should only be done with the candidate's agreement and if it is in the candidate's best interests to do so.

The only time confidentiality should be breached is when the person is at significant risk – particularly those aged under 18.

Case study Lianne Davis, freelance assessor

'While working for a private training provider, I had a concern about a female candidate who was doing the Level 2 award. Her work within her placement was excellent and the staff there were very happy with her progress, as was I. However, her attendance became very erratic, with her often missing days in a row. Upon challenging her about this, she confided in me that her mother had taken an overdose, so she had to stay at home while her father was on day shifts. It was obviously a very distressing time for the candidate, and I assured her that I would maintain her confidentiality. She informed me that her mother was getting help and that the family was attending group counselling, so I was happy that she was getting the support she needed. I spoke to her placement supervisor and explained that, while I could not divulge the reasons for the candidate's erratic attendance due to confidentiality, I could assure her that the reasons were genuine and would hopefully get better with time. The candidate felt supported but not interrogated and was soon back to her normal attendance patterns.'

Confidentiality

The control of the spread of information that is inappropriate to disseminate or share.

Keys to good practice
Confidentiality

- Do not gossip about candidates or their families, either inside or outside the workplace.
- Never give candidates' contact details to others without their consent, unless requested by the emergency services.
- Keep written information in a safe place.
- If you are unsure about whether you have the authority to pass on information, always check with your line manager or the candidate themselves.

Adapted from *Children's Care, Learning and Development, Level 3,* P Tassoni, K Bulman, K Beith, M Robinson, p.14.

Over to you!
Confidentiality

Consider how your centre maintains the confidentiality of its candidates. How is information stored and is this effective? Does your centre have a confidentiality policy and, if so, how effective is it?

Relationship with candidates

The roles of assessor and candidate are fairly straightforward, but it is important that the rules of the relationship are clearly defined. You are an expert providing a service to candidates,

so you should treat them with respect and concern. You will want to find out about their personal interests and background in order to consider all aspects of their learning requirements. It is essential, therefore, that you find the balance between professionalism and personal friendship. You should strive to be close enough to your candidates to be helpful and friendly, while not crossing the professional boundaries you have set.

Helping candidates move forward

Many candidates will have their own comfort zone in which they feel safe and secure and able to live happily. However, you should encourage learners to move beyond this zone and to take risks and face uncertainty, in order to move forward in their education, training and career. This can be done by working through a SWOT analysis with your candidates. A SWOT analysis identifies strengths, weaknesses, opportunities and threats. Encouraging candidates to identify these things can make their pathways clearer. Table 1 shows an example of SWOT analysis questions.

Table 1   SWOT analysis questions

Strengths	Weaknesses
What do you do well? What do you see as your strengths? What do others see as your strengths?	Where could you improve? What do you think are your weaker areas? What are others likely to see as weaknesses?
Opportunities	Threats
What good opportunities are available to you? How could you turn your strengths into opportunities?	What threats do your weaknesses expose you to? What might stand in your way of taking advantage of your opportunities?

Completing a SWOT analysis with your candidates helps them to look at themselves and the opportunities available to them. You might find it useful to carry it out again after perhaps six months, to see how they have made changes.

This move forward, however, cannot be done unless the candidate trusts and respects you and your judgements. If a candidate does not feel they have a secure and reliable relationship with you, they will be more likely to resist the learning process you are putting in place, and therefore not be actively engaged in their own learning.

Building relationships with candidates

The beginning of a new training course is, for many candidates, an exciting time, providing new experiences and learning opportunities. Your candidates will be enthusiastic, creative and open to new ideas. However, it is also a daunting situation, with unfamiliar people and places, as well as transitional problems and new challenges. Building relationships with your candidates from the onset of their training is vital if you are to provide them with the fullest support and guidance, and there are many ways to achieve this throughout their time with you.

Effective relationships are ones built around mutual trust and respect. Your candidates will rely on your knowledge and professional judgement to open the pathways to their learning, and look upon you as their mentor and guide as well as their assessor. You will need to trust them to work in a professional manner while on placement and representing their training centre and to inform you in advance of assessment opportunities or any concerns they may have. Respect for each other is essential if a relationship is to be formed. It is inevitable that you may not always see eye to eye with candidates; however, you should always respect your candidates' wishes, and develop positive open relationships, where candidates feel able to communicate with you.

Initial contact

Your initial contact with your candidate will depend on how your centre works. In many training establishments, it is the assessor who carries out the interviews with potential candidates, so you may well be the person who has the initial contact with the candidate. Being involved in the interview stage of enrolment allows you to gather information about your candidates from the outset, giving you the opportunity to ensure that you can offer training that is suited to the individual needs of the candidate. First impressions really do count and you will most likely find that candidates are eager to portray a positive image of themselves and their experiences. This interview time provides the ideal opportunity to get to know the basics about your candidate and you may find it helpful to have a list of interview questions ready to ensure that you get the most from the time available. It may be that your centre has a dedicated interview person, in which case you should liaise closely with them, explaining the information you would like them to find out about your candidates and perhaps give them a list of questions you would like them to ask.

> **Over to you!**
> Initial contact
>
> Make a list of questions you might ask potential candidates at interview.

> **Over to you!**
> New training
>
> If you were a candidate embarking on a new training course, what would you want the assessor to ask you with regard to your needs? What sorts of things would you need to know from the assessor, and what would they need to know about you?

Empowering candidates

Empowering candidates to believe in their abilities and dreams is an essential part of the relationship building process. A candidate needs to feel you believe in them and that you have confidence in them as an able person. How the relationship develops will depend on the candidate's previous experiences, and the relationships they have had in the past with school teachers and mentors, for example.

> **Over to you!**
> Relationships with teachers/lecturers
>
> Consider the relationships you formed with teachers or lecturers at school or college. What kind of impact have these relationships had on you and on your ability to build relationships for yourself?

Case study Rachel Meredith

Rachel Meredith is a full-time S/NVQ candidate at her local further education college. She is in her first year of her Level 2 programme.

'I was fine at primary school and got on well with the teachers and other staff, but things changed when I moved into secondary school. I found the workload hard going and when my mum and dad split up, I went through a hard time. I began to skip lessons and, because I missed so much work, I found it difficult in the classes I did attend. I got a bit of a reputation for being rude to the teachers and I acted that way because I felt that that was what they expected of me. I left school without many qualifications, but I always wanted to work with young children. I wasn't sure if my school reputation and my lack of qualifications would make it difficult for me to get into college, but the idea of work-based learning really appealed to me. When I met my assessor, she was clear about what was expected of me, and told me that placements would not put up with me missing my work days, but she also said that she wanted me to make a fresh start, and she treated me like an adult. She wasn't at all like I expected, I thought she would be like the teachers at school, but she had respect for me and I didn't want to let her, or myself, down. She makes time to ask me how my personal life is, and I only have to tell her the things I want her to know – she isn't nosey, but I know I can talk to her about things other than my training, and she doesn't judge me. If I'm not pulling my weight or getting my work done on time, she explains to me what I can do to improve rather than telling me off. I love the S/NVQ course because I'm doing something I really want to do, and I really like my assessor. I can't wait to complete this Level 2 as my placement supervisor has said they will employ me full time, and then I can carry on to do my Level 3.'

Think about...

1. Why do you think Rachel has found the work-based learning route more successful?
2. How has her assessor built a successful relationship with Rachel?

Building appropriate relationships

As you get to know your individual candidates, you will begin to judge the type of relationship that is appropriate. Some candidates will be self-motivated and will not require as much of your time, understanding their requirements, and handing in their work regularly. Others, however, may need more input from you and require a higher level of support. You should use your professional judgement to decide on the appropriateness of your time allocation to a particular candidate, while ensuring that the more confident candidates also get an equal amount of your time.

Above all, relationships with your candidates should be individual to their needs and should always demonstrate mutual respect, honesty and trust.

Over to you!
Building appropriate relationships

Read the following descriptions of imaginary candidates and consider how you would build appropriate relationships with each one.

1 Emily is a confident 16-year-old. She enjoyed school and was successful in her exams. She has a supportive family and attends placement regularly.

2 Rani is from a close-knit family and her parents are not sure she is ready to be in a work environment. She is a friendly girl, quiet and personable, with few friends.

3 Paula is very outgoing and loud and has little respect for others around her. She sometimes feels as if the world is against her and often goes into her placement in 'sulky moods', moaning about her boyfriend.

Supporting candidates with additional needs

In Chapter 1, you looked at the barriers to learning and employment and training and the strategies set out to improve this within the Children's Workforce Development Strategy (see pages 12–19). Your candidates will come in all shapes and sizes with varying needs and abilities and from a variety of backgrounds and communities.

Access to assessment

Planning assessment opportunities with your candidates allows them to take ownership of their own learning, dictating the speed of their own training, while allowing you to encourage, support and guide the candidate. The style of assessment planning will be individual to your candidates; however, it is essential that all of your candidates have equal access to assessment and are treated with equal concern. The CCLD assessment strategy sets out guidelines for access to assessment, detailing how 'all candidates should be offered appropriate support to enable them to access assessment'. It is important that your centre works within the boundaries of codes of practice and relevant legislation, such as the Disability Discrimination Act 1995 and the Data Protection Act 1998.

In Chapter 1, you saw the kinds of barrier people face when attempting to access training and employment, such as racism and sexism (see pages 14–17). Your role as an assessor is to ensure that these barriers are challenged and procedures are put in place to support candidates with additional needs. Where mechanisms have been put in place for such support, it is also essential that the candidate is not given, or appears to have been given, an unfair advantage. You should always aim to support the individual needs of your candidates, while maintaining the integrity and quality of the award.

Check it out

You can obtain a copy of the CCLD assessment strategy at www.cwdcouncil.org.uk

Anti-discriminatory practice

Taking action to counter discrimination, identifying and challenging discrimination

---

Case study Lynsdale Community College

This small community college prides itself on its inclusive ethos. Each candidate is accepted onto a course on their own merit, not on the outcome of their GCSE results. The sector manager for the childcare team states:

'We interview each candidate individually and ask them to carry out an initial assessment, which includes basic skills. It is important to stress that the results from this assessment do not determine whether the candidate is accepted, but informs our decisions of appropriate support. A candidate may not be very good at maths, but if we can see the potential and desire to learn in the candidate, then we are prepared to give them a chance. We have various support mechanisms in place, depending on the needs of the candidate. For example, we have counsellors and support workers who might work with candidates who have personal issues, translators and interpreters for students with English as a second language, facilitators for the deaf, scribing, note-taking and specialist computer equipment. We are extremely proud of the facilities and resources available, and even more pleased to see candidates with particular support needs growing in confidence and achieving qualifications that will help them on the road to employment.'

Earlier in this chapter, you thought about the kinds of questions you might ask a potential candidate during an interview (see page 41). When interviewing candidates with additional needs there is some basic information you need to find out, in order to ensure that the interview is appropriate for them. For example, if the candidate is a wheelchair user, you may need to make alternative access arrangements, or have

a translator available for an interview with a candidate who has English as their second language. All of this information should be on the candidate's application form and it is important that you consider any information provided on the form carefully, making positive arrangements and ensuring **anti-discriminatory practice**. Ensuring the appropriate arrangements are made will not only allow the interview to run smoothly, but will also demonstrate the provider's commitment to equality and diversity and allow the candidate to feel that their individual needs are recognised and important, therefore empowering the candidate and making the interview more relaxed.

Should a candidate have a specific requirement, it will be useful for you to gather as much information about this as possible, and find out the support available both within your centre and locally, to help the candidate engage in learning.

Inclusion

Identifying, understanding and breaking down barriers to participation and belonging

Check it out

You can find out more about supporting candidates with disabilities at www.skill.org.uk

Over to you!
Inclusive assessment opportunities

In order to ensure you provide inclusive assessment opportunities, you may need to alter the way you support and guide candidates. Read through the scenarios below, and consider the strategies you may implement for each candidate, on the basis of their individual needs.

1 You have a Level 2 female candidate with a visual impairment.
2 You have a Level 3 candidate who has a history of self-harm due to bullying. She has not self-harmed over the last eight months since leaving school and beginning college.
3 You have a male candidate with dyslexia coming for an interview for the Level 2 course.

Case study Rathbone

Rathbone is an education and training provider working in Scotland, England and Wales. Operating from 70 centres and projects, Rathbone supports over 12,000 young people and adults every year and employs 1,000 staff. Rathbone is dedicated to working with young people who very often have not been successful in their secondary education. Many such young people require access to education and training opportunities that are tailored specifically to their learning and social support needs. At Rathbone, every attempt is made to personalise the support provided in order to enable each of their clients to receive the most out of their time there. They are also committed to supporting young people who are excluded from school. Rathbone also works with young people who are subject to the provisions of the youth justice system. Rathbone staff have been at the forefront of innovative initiatives to encourage young people who are not in education, employment or training to recommit to positive activities. Seven out of ten of those with whom they work in this way progress into positive further training or education outcomes. Rathbone provides a wide range of services nationwide, including:

- education and training programmes to:
  - support the government's Entry to Employment (E2E) initiative
  - help young people into apprenticeship programmes
  - retrain adults who have been unemployed long term so they can get back into work

- programmes to support young people in inner cities who have fallen out of mainstream education
- special programmes for young people under 16 who have been excluded from school or are in danger of being excluded
- a Special Education Advice Line (SEAL) that supports young people and their families and carers who are having difficulty finding the right education for their particular needs.

Within the childcare and early years team, they specifically work to build confidence and self-esteem issues. Many of the candidates have a lot to offer children, and have very caring and nurturing personalities. Their job as S/NVQ assessors is not only to guide the candidates through the S/NVQ, but also to draw out the candidates' strengths and empower them to believe they can achieve their goals and aspirations.

Above all, it is important to treat all candidates with equal concern and as individuals, supporting their needs and ensuring they have the opportunities to maximise their potential.

Ensuring differentiation between candidates

Throughout this book, we look at the importance of treating all candidates as individuals and with equal concern. **Differentiation** is the process of adjusting your teaching, assessing and learning methods according to the learning needs of your candidates. The way you differentiate between your candidates may be as a whole **cohort**, as smaller groups within that cohort or as an individual candidate.

Differentiation can be split into categories, for example:

- by task – identifying appropriate tasks for candidates depending on their different ability levels
- by outcome – providing opportunities for candidates to do the same activity with different levels of response
- by support – providing differing levels of support or help within the same cohort.

Check it out

You can find out more about the work of Rathbone at www.rathboneuk.org

Differentiation

There are many different definitions of differentiation. Ofsted defines it as 'the matching of work to the differing capabilities of individuals or groups of pupils in order to extend their learning'.

Cohort

A group of individuals having a factor in common.

Over to you!
Methods of differentiation

Think about your previous work with young children. Identify the methods you used to differentiate between the children you worked with, and how these strategies might be used with your S/NVQ candidates.

Meeting the varying needs within a group

In order to successfully differentiate between your candidates, you need to recognise that all candidates are different. They may:

- have specific needs, abilities and disabilities
- have different prior knowledge, experience and skills
- work and learn at different speeds
- have differing levels of confidence
- find some aspects of their programme difficult or easy
- have particular interests
- have a preference for different methods and styles of learning.

Learning styles

As your relationships with your candidates grow and develop, you will appreciate their differences in opinions, approaches and learning styles. These learning styles can be defined in a number of ways, as Table 2 demonstrates.

Table 2   Different learning styles

Learning style	Description
Auditory	Auditory learners learn best by hearing information, such as during a lecture. They respond well by talking things through with others, and listening to their response. **Key words:** Listen, hear, talk, debate, recite, discuss, dialogue, repetition
Visual	Visual learners learn by seeing, through film, demonstration and video, for example. **Key words:** See, watch, imagine, picture, visualise, draw, look, display
Kinaesthetic	Kinaesthetic learners learn in a practical way, such as by experimentation or acting out a scene. **Key words:** Sensation, do, touch, feel, move, act, take, get, experience
Multi-sensory	Multi-sensory learners learn best by listening, seeing and doing – that is, all of the above types of learning mixed together. They prefer to have all the types together to give a full picture of the learning outcome. **Key words:** Listen, watch, do, hear, see, feel, talk, imagine, sensation, debate, act, visualise, experience, recite, dramatise, picture, discuss, display, get, formulate, draw, dialogue, clear sight, touch, repetition

One of the biggest challenges for assessors of vocational learning is how to respond to these differences across a cohort. It is essential that you understand the diversity of your candidates and look at ways to engage them all, rather than adopting a one-size-fits-all approach.

When preparing training and learning sessions for your candidates, you should consider:

- how to include a variety of learning activities, from cut-and-stick to use of interactive whiteboards
- how the session may work with a variety of learning styles
- how the activities will promote contributions from all candidates
- how you will ensure that higher-ability candidates are challenged and stimulated
- how the less-confident candidates will be encouraged and supported
- the processes you will use to determine the outcomes of the session
- how you will assess the candidates' progress
- how initial assessment may identify learning needs.

Over to you!
Strategies to engage different learning styles

Think about your candidate group and their individual learning styles. Make a list of strategies you could use to engage them in activities, while differentiating across the group.

Table 3 Activities for differentiation

Activity	Description	Example	Differentiation
Open questioning	Ask your candidates an open question and to work on this individually or in pairs for a few minutes. You should then ask them if they have an answer and support them if they found the task too difficult. It is important that you choose who gives the answers, rather than asking for a volunteer, to avoid getting the same confident candidate answering all the time.	'Jane and Louise, could you think about the impact that a relationship breakdown might have on a child in your care? I'll give you five minutes to think about it and then I'd like Louise to feed your thoughts back to the rest of the group.'	You will be able to gauge from this the level at which the candidates have understanding on the subject, based on the depth and breadth of the answer they provide, and the methods they use to conclude their answers.
Group work	Candidates work in small groups for a few minutes to answer a question or complete a task set by you. You then ask the groups if they have an answer and help those that do not or that ask for help. Again, you should ask an individual for the answer, not leave it up to a volunteer.	'OK, you guys on the back table, could you use the magazines to find a range of gross motor play activities for a group of 2–4-year-old children? If you could cut them out and stick them onto A4 sheets, I can then get them photocopied so everyone has one. Liam, could you then feed back please?'	From this activity, you can observe how well the groups work together and encourage any candidates who may be getting left behind or are not engaged. The practical side of the activity allows visual or kinaesthetic learners to become fully engaged.

Activity	Description	Example	Differentiation
Create it!	Ask your candidates to become creative and produce leaflets, handouts, books, even children's toys. This can be done alone, in pairs, or in small or large groups.	'I want you to imagine that you are the new manager of a private day nursery. You need to produce a handbook to give to prospective parents to inform them of the ethos, policies and practices of the setting. You can work together on this, but you must produce a handbook each.'	Again, visual and kinaesthetic learners will really enjoy this. This activity allows your candidates to produce something that is entirely their own, and to explore their ideas and practices, giving you indications of their abilities, knowledge and skills.
Essays and assignments	This may be when you give all candidates a set task to complete alone and in a set style or format within a given brief.	'I want you all to write a 2,000 word essay as follows. Describe what is meant by the term anti-discriminatory practice, and discuss how this is implemented within your setting. Evaluate its effectiveness, and demonstrate your commitment to its meaning.'	This type of activity will demonstrate a candidate's ability to work on their own initiative and produce work in accordance with a brief within a set timescale. You can determine the level of understanding the candidate has and how they contextualise this understanding within their work setting.

(Continued)

Table 3 (*Continued*)

Activity	Description	Example	Differentiation
Worksheets	Give your candidates worksheets with a range of measured questions. The questions get harder as the candidate moves on. You could offer extension activities for the higher-ability candidates.	'I want you all to work through this worksheet at your own pace. Leave out any questions that you are unsure of and return to them at the end.'	Worksheets are an ideal way of understanding the level that candidates are working at and also looking at the different capabilities and understanding of the mix of candidates within the group. Allowing them to mark each other's, or their own as a group, will offer them the opportunity to learn from each other and support each other.
Formative tests and quizzes	Ask your candidates a variety of questions that you have pre-determined, in accordance with your planning and learning strategies.	'Right then everyone, we are going to have a fun quiz… Number 1: A child is sitting at a table, cutting out shapes from a catalogue. What skills will this activity be helping him to develop? Number 2…'	This allows your candidates to establish which questions they got wrong and work on these within class time. You may find that there is a common area of misunderstanding that you should do more work on or that the candidates have actually understood more than you originally thought!

Activity	Description	Example	Differentiation
Experiment/practical	This kind of activity allows candidates to be practical, make mistakes and make choices.	'On the table at the front I have a range of sterilisation methods, a variety of bottles and teats and different forms of powdered milk. I would like you all to have a go at the different sterilisation methods and making up a bottle feed.'	The practicality of this task makes it fun and real. You will have the opportunity to observe how well the candidates work together and share the resources, possibly helping each other out and learning from each other.
Case studies	Candidates are given a variety of case studies with measured questions. The varying degree of questions will enable all of your candidates to take part.	'I will give you all the same set of case studies. In groups, read through them and think about your responses to the questions at the end. I would then like a member from each group to feed back their answers to the rest of us.'	This kind of activity will allow you to see the differentiation of confidence in the group. Almost immediately, you will see the 'authoritarians' reading out the case studies to the rest of their groups and then deciding how the responses will be noted. These people will also probably be the ones who feed back the answers to the others.
Presentations	Give pairs or small groups of candidates a topic that they must research and present to the rest of the group.	'. . . Group 3, I would like you to research multiple sclerosis and its effects on the family . . .'	Allowing candidates to present their own findings will allow them to work at their own pace and level, while providing you with opportunities to assess their skills, levels and capabilities.

Over to you!
Activities for differentiation

Take a look at the following activity notes sheet and consider how it provides a range of activities to cover the subject matter. Can you see how the activities vary to include a variety of the learning styles in Table 3?

Table 4 Activity notes sheet

Activity	Activity notes
1 **Short answer** **Cloze activity** Safety marks	Candidates work on their own to identify safety marks and complete a cloze activity.
2 **Wordsearch** **Discussion** Hazards	Following individual completion of the wordsearch, candidates then work in small groups to discuss their strategies for managing the listed hazards and also to share their workplace procedures for these hazards.
3 **Research** Adult:child ratios	If you have copies you may wish to use the Guidance to the Care Standards Act (Standard 2) to help the group to research this. If not, you could carry out Task 2 first and discuss the correct ratio in advance. Tasks 3 and 4 would then follow after 1 in this case.
4 **Group discussion** Equipment checks and storage	You should carry out group discussion about safety checks before asking candidates to complete the tasks.
5 **Individual exercises** Safety equipment	You may wish to brainstorm safety equipment ideas before candidates complete these tasks.
6 **Various** Safety indoors	Encourage the sharing of workplace experiences. Carry out the activity in pairs, so that the discussion can inform those with less experience. For Task 2, you may need to explain the 'triad of impairment' before candidates look at the case study. You could show the PowerPoint® presentation about autistic spectrum disorders.

Over to you!
Activities for differentiation

Activity	Activity notes
7 **Various** **Case study** Emergency procedures	You will need to ask candidates to bring in their workplace safety and emergency procedures so that you can discuss their similarities and differences. Task 3 requires candidates to discuss the statements after they have completed their answers. This activity will help them to rationalise their choices and decisions. If new to their workplace, they may need to refer to the policies and procedures. Task 7 may be best completed once candidates have completed some first aid training.
8 **Wordsearch** **Case study** **True/false** Behaviour management	Before this activity is started, talk about how behaviour is managed and what each of the terms means. The PowerPoint® presentation gives information about five behavioural theorists and explains the terms used in the wordsearch. Tasks 2, 3 and 4 should each be discussed in small groups once candidates have completed them.
9 **Group activity** **Individual revision exercise** Safety on outings	Task 1 is quite complex. You might like to look at the suggested answers (on the CD-ROM) and perhaps copy them onto cards to distribute among the group for discussion first. The cards could then be sorted into a planning order – preparation, organisation, the outing itself. You might also want to discuss the importance of reviewing the safety arrangements afterwards to see if any improvements might be made. Task 2 should be completed as a revision exercise to show transferability of information.

(Continued)

Over to you!
Activities for differentiation

Table 4 *(Continued)*

Activity		Activity notes
10	**Research task** Signs of illness	You may wish to provide textbooks for Task 1. The PowerPoint® presentation gives details about meningitis.
11	**Cloze activity** Hygiene	Before giving out this activity, lead a group discussion on what is meant by cross-infection. Candidates then work in pairs to discuss how germs spread from one person to another. Task 2 is an individual gap-fill activity about how to avoid cross-infection.

Source: *S/NVQ Level 2 Children's Care, Learning and Development, Knowledge and Evidence Resource File*, Heinemann, 2005, p.41

The key message to take from this chapter is that you need to build appropriate trusting relationships, through which your knowledge of the candidates informs how you work with them to achieve the best possible outcome.

Check your understanding

As you have reached the end of this chapter, you may find it useful to consolidate all that you have learnt by answering the following questions. You will find suggested answers in the back of the book on page 174.

1   What are the three foundations to any relationship?
2   What is meant by 'confidentiality'?
3   Which Act governs the storage of confidential information?
4   Why is it important to understand your candidates' prior learning experiences?
5   Why is the CCLD assessment strategy important?
6   List three ways in which you could ensure equality of opportunity.
7   What is meant by 'anti-discriminatory practice'?
8   What does the term 'differentiation' mean?
9   Why is differentiation important?
10   How would a multi-sensory learner learn best?

Chapter **3**

Assessment processes

Introduction

The terms *collecting evidence* and *evidence gathering* are used by many assessors throughout the S/NVQ process; however, it is important not to take them too literally. Your candidates' portfolios are more than folders of evidence; they should demonstrate your candidates' abilities, skills, knowledge and competencies required by the National Occupational Standards (NOS). Assessment of candidates' competence will be your main role as an assessor. With an emphasis on high-quality assessments of actual work practice, you will support and guide your candidates through the whole process, offering them ideas about how to demonstrate their competence and evidence their skills and abilities.

This chapter aims to introduce you to the many types of assessment opportunity open to you and your candidates within the Children's Care, Learning and Development (CCLD) NOS. You will consider how planning for assessment and learning takes place and the requirements for diagnostic screening and initial assessment.

This chapter will help you to understand:
- the range of assessment opportunities available
- how to plan effective assessment opportunities
- how to judge evidence and provide feedback
- e-portfolios.

The range of assessment opportunities available

Candidates need to demonstrate their competence in skills relating to the National Occupational Standards (NOS) in Children's Care, Learning and Development (CCLD). This demonstration can take many forms, depending on the opportunities available to each candidate. Assessment of candidates should determine whether or not their performance meets the defined standards, as well as the validity, authenticity and sufficiency of that evidence.

Collecting evidence should be a two-way process, with the responsibility divided between you and the candidate. You will take responsibility for collating and structuring the evidence, according to the portfolio house style determined by your training centre. You will carry out the direct observations and facilitate the professional discussion, referencing both accordingly and supplementing them with questioning. The candidates will take responsibility for gathering supplementary evidence, particularly for units that are difficult to be directly observed. Your candidates should also take responsibility for informing you of any one-off assessment opportunities, such as special events that might provide rare assessment opportunities. By working with your candidates, their portfolios will be evidence-rich and streamlined to hold only the necessary information.

Within the CCLD NOS, you will find a list of evidence gathering methods that describes the ways in which candidates can demonstrate their competence for the award. These are:

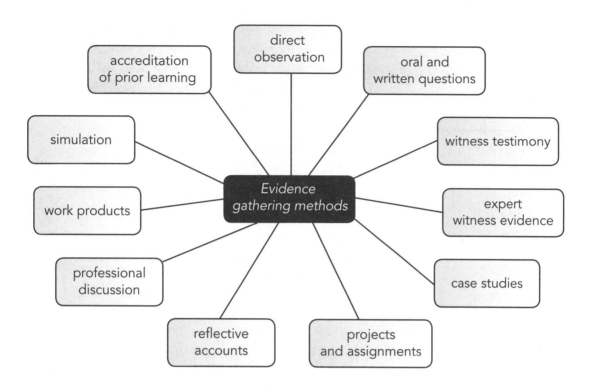

Direct observation

'Assessing holistically' is a term used to describe a method for assessing a candidate's performance in the workplace. **Holistic assessment** involves the assessor and the candidate looking at a forthcoming event at the candidate's workplace and deciding where this evidence could fit into a range of units and elements within the NOS. Working in this holistic manner allows the evidence to be generated from real work situations, rather than the candidate 'setting up' activities with the children to cover a particular unit or element.

An example of holistic assessment might be during outside play. The assessor would arrange to see the candidate supporting children during the outside play session, with a brief idea of the kind of evidence she might see that candidate perform. However, the assessor would not specify to the candidate exactly what she should do, rather she would allow the situation to develop as it normally would. By working in this manner, the assessor could observe the candidate carrying out a range of activities with the children, such as working with a child to provide emotional support and developing behavioural strategies. She might be involved in first aid or be playing group games with the children.

> **Holistic assessment**
> Observing real work situations as they happen with a view to covering a range of units and elements.

The opposite of this holistic approach would be for the assessor to specify to the candidate that the candidate should play a game of 'Farmer's in the Den' with a group of children. This specificity means that other sources of observational evidence could well be missed.

> ## Direct observation
>
> A record of the actions performed by the candidate during real work situations

Holistic **direct observation** should be the primary source of evidence for your candidates. During direct observations, you will be watching a candidate carrying out their normal duties within their setting and writing the observation as you see it happen (often referred to as 'naturally occurring evidence').

Assessing holistically also means looking at the whole picture of what the candidate is doing, rather than focusing on a particular task, activity or unit of the NOS. A holistic observation will detail how the candidate has shown competency, covering a range of Performance Criteria within a variety of units and elements. Assessing holistically allows observations to be comprehensive and easily cross-referenced, capturing the naturally occurring evidence demonstrated by the candidate under real work conditions.

Once the observation has been written, the assessor will then cross-reference it by identifying which Performance Criteria and Knowledge Specifications have been demonstrated from which units, and cross-referencing them with the NOS. Cross-referencing is something that gets easier with practice. It is a means of relating what you have seen the candidate do, and written in your observation, to the requirements of the NOS. For example, you might have written the following statement within an observation of a Level 3 candidate.

> '. . . Sarah then encouraged the child to discuss the picture she had made, allowing the child time to express herself. Sarah praised the child verbally, telling her how hard she had worked and how proud she was of her. Sarah then asked the child if it would be OK to put her picture on the display board so that all the children could see it . . .'

Once you have completed writing the observation, you would then decide how this evidence demonstrated competence towards the NOS. For example, you might cross-reference the above statement to the following Performance Criteria.

Table 1 Cross-referencing direct observation

Unit	PC/Knowledge Specification	
301	301.1, 1	Interact with children in a way that helps them feel welcome and valued
301	301.2, 1	Communicate with children in a way that is appropriate to their ages, needs and abilities
301	301.2, 2	Listen to children and respond to them in a way that shows that you value what they say and feel
301	K3D164	The importance of involving children in decision making and strategies you can use to do this

Over to you!
Cross-referencing direct observation

Take a look at the following direct observation. Consider which units of Level 2 CCLD the candidate has demonstrated competence for and try to reference it to the Performance Criteria. Some have already been done for you as an example.

Whitmore Community College
Direct Observation Sheet

Name of Candidate: Najma Begum

Specific Considerations: Najma working with mixed ability group of children aged 2-3 years. One child with learning difficulties

Name of Assessor: Mary Foxhall

Placement: Smarties Play Group

Observation Date: Monday 19ᵗʰ May 2006

Time: 10 am

Direct Observation Details	Unit	PC	KS
On arrival at the playgroup, I was greeted at the door by Najma (N), who asked me to sign in and ensured the door was closed properly behind me. N then escorted me to the main playroom where she had prepared a table top activity for a group of mixed gender, mixed ability children aged 2-3 years. N informed me that one child (A) had specific learning difficulties and found it hard to concentrate. She told me that the child's care plan stated that the child was to be encouraged to stay at the activity for as long as she could, but to allow her the freedom to leave the activity when she felt it was appropriate. N had prepared a picture lotto game, which she informed me was to develop concentration and matching skills, as well as social skills such as turn taking. The table had been prepared in a quiet corner of the room, away from distractions of other activities taking place. The table and chairs were of an appropriate size for the children participating. N gathered a group of 4 children, asking if they would like to play the game; one child was the child mentioned earlier with learning difficulties (A). N helped the children to sit at the table, and explained the rules to them, using language that was appropriate to their developmental stages, and asking the children to repeat the rules back to her to ensure they understood. N praised the children for sitting nicely and began the game. N asked the children to each take a card and look at the pictures on it. She asked each child in turn what pictures they had, requesting for other children to wait their turn, and listen to what the children were saying. She allowed each child sufficient time to communicate, and responded appropriately, using positive facial expressions, and verbal praise. She praised the children for their discussion. As the lotto cards were turned over, N asked each child to check to see if it matched their card. She also used descriptive words for the pictures including big, little, smaller, on top, and asked the children to name the colours of the objects. Throughout the activity, N praised the children for their efforts, and encouraged social skills. Child (A) began to get restless, and took the card from the child beside her, making the child cry. N intervened straight away, comforting the crying child, whilst asking A to give the card back to the child. N explained to A that it wasn't nice to take from other children, and that this behaviour had upset another child. A gave the card back and N asked A to say sorry to the child, which she did. N then continued with the game, holding the child's interest until the end of the activity.	202.3 202.1 202.1 202.1	2 1 3 4	 K2C1

You can also observe **work products** as evidence (**product evidence**). For example, while carrying out a direct observation, your candidate might show you an accident record book, demonstrating how she dealt with an accident and recorded it according to the policies and procedures of the setting. You should then write this within your direct observation, stating that you have seen the document and that it was completed accurately. It would not be necessary for the candidate to include copies of this document as evidence within their portfolio as you have stated that you have seen it, and used your professional judgement to decide its value as evidence.

Professional discussion

The CCLD S/NVQ lends itself very well to the use of **professional discussion**. This alternative method of presenting evidence enables you to understand why your candidate performed in a particular way. Professional discussions are a useful tool for drawing depth and breadth of knowledge and help candidates to reflect on their practice, providing an opportunity for them to discuss how they feel their practice and evidence meets the NOS. As an assessment tool, it can be one of the most effective ways of ensuring the validity and reliability of candidates' evidence.

Professional discussions can be recorded in a range of formats, including on tape or in writing, and should be in the form of a structured review of candidates' practice. They are particularly useful in demonstrating what candidates know, and how well they understand the Principles and Values of the childcare sector. You should encourage your candidates to reflect on how they have demonstrated their commitment to the policies within their setting and to external legislation, critically evaluating their practice.

There are three key stages to professional discussion:

1 planning the discussion
2 carrying out the discussion
3 recording and evidencing the discussion.

1 Planning the discussion

It is important that both you and the candidate are clear about the reasons behind and the anticipated outcomes of the discussion. You will need to consider which elements of the NOS you want to cover, particularly if there are gaps in the

> **Work products**
> Evidence produced by the candidate themselves during work practice.
>
> **Product evidence**
> Products derived from real work situations, such as fire drill records, accident books, stationery orders, etc.

> **Professional discussion**
> A discussion between the candidate and the assessor to draw depth and breadth of knowledge and understanding and establish the rationale behind the candidate's actions.

evidence that could be met by discussion with the candidate. You should then note the points you want to discuss and provide a copy of these to your candidate in advance of the discussion. This will allow the candidate to research any information that might be required and also to consider any further evidence they might bring with them to the discussion to visually support their evidence. How this plan is presented will vary from centre to centre, but it may look something like this:

Assessment Plan

Award: NVQ Level 2 in CCLD   **Date:** 25th May 2006

Candidate's Name: Mandy Hargreaves   **Candidate PIN No:** 123456

Assessor's Name: Josephine Banks

Evidence to be gathered	Date	By whom	Achieved
Holistic observation within the pre-school setting	22/09/05	Josephine Banks	
Professional discussion	22/09/05	Josephine Banks and Mandy Hargreaves	
Witness testimony on dealing with waste	28/09/05	Mrs Ashen	
Reflective account supporting children with personal safety	28/09/05	Mandy Hargreaves	

---

2 Carrying out the discussion

The candidate should feel comfortable and at ease during the discussion and should be allowed plenty of time to consider their views and express their opinions. They should also be given the opportunity to ask questions about anything they are unsure of and to comment accordingly. Your role will be to facilitate the discussion, prompting when necessary, without leading or directing the candidate in any way. It should not be a question and answer session, but rather a conversation led by the candidate in order for them to demonstrate their knowledge and understanding.

3 Recording and evidencing the discussion

It is a requirement that you make an audio recording of the professional discussion, as this will ensure that nothing is missed when referencing the evidence. The referencing of professional discussions needs to be clear and accurate. Table 2 shows an example of how taped evidence may be referenced.

Table 2 Referencing taped evidence

Tape counter number	Topic of discussion	NOS requirements met
1–13	Setting in-house training on inclusion and equality attended by candidate on 04/03/06	305.1 – 3, 4, 6, 7 305.2 – 1, 2, 4, 5, 6, 7 K3P233, K3P234, K3P235, K3D237, K3D239, K3P241, K3D243, K3P1121, K3S249
14–27	Discussed how the above training has improved candidate's practice, knowledge and skills	304.1 – 1, 2, 3, 4, 6 304.2 – 1, 3, 4 K3P222, K3D223, K3D224, K3D225, K3D227, K3P229, K3P231, K3M232

> ## Case study Sandwell College
>
> The early years and childcare sector of the college has recently introduced the use of MP3 recorders to record professional discussions. They stated:
>
> 'We are slowly but surely bringing the sector up to date with new technology and our long-term goal is the introduction of electronic portfolios. The use of MP3 recorders is one step closer to this aim, and has been well received within the college. When a candidate and assessor have a professional discussion, it is recorded via the MP3 recorders. The assessor then uploads the recording onto a computer, where it remains saved so that it can be verified by the internal or external verifier, as required. The assessor then references the discussion on log sheets as they normally would. This method enables the assessor to be clear about the candidate's knowledge and skills, and releases them from the time spent writing the discussion down as they have previously.'

Using digital recordings may allow for further accuracy in the referencing of the discussion and make the sourcing of the evidence easier. (See the section on e-portfolios, on pages 81–84, for more information about this.)

Oral and written questions

Questioning can be used as an effective way to check your candidate's understanding. You may find that during direct observations the candidate does something in particular about which you would like to clarify their understanding. For example, you might be observing your candidate during sand play, when he asks one child to wear gloves. It would not be appropriate to interrupt the candidate during the observation to ask why he has done this, so you might make a note to ask him at the end. If the candidate's response was appropriate (for example, if the child had a skin complaint that was aggravated by the sand), you would be able to reference his understanding accordingly. However, if the candidate did not know why he had done this and/or, for example, only did it because he saw other practitioners doing so, this would not show competency and you might set him a task or ask him to research the information further.

Questioning

Using questions to clarify the knowledge and understanding of the candidate.

Closed question

A question that can be answered with either a single word or a short phrase, such as 'Yes' or 'No'.

Open question

A question that allows a longer answer, giving the candidate control of the conversation.

Questions can also be used when direct observation is not available, such as within *Unit 303*. As this unit looks at observations of children's development, it may not be appropriate for you to observe, and therefore you might ask a candidate questions about why she carried out an observation, why she chose a particular method and how she would use the observation of the child for forward planning. Another example is within *Unit 302*, where it is unlikely that you will observe an emergency, and therefore you might question the candidate with 'what if' situations. Questions can be asked verbally and the responses written down by you, or they can be pre-written and given to the candidate to complete, whichever is most appropriate for you and your candidate. You could even make an audio recording of the questions and answers.

Keys to good practice
Asking verbal questions

- Choose the right time.
- Use testing questions (questions that check the understanding of the candidate) starting with *who, what, why, when* and *how*.
- Encourage the candidate to clarify the answer, for example, by asking, 'What did you mean by . . .?', 'Can you give me an example of that?'
- Encourage the candidate to expand on their answer, for example, by asking, 'How did that make you feel?', 'Can you tell me more about that?'
- Encourage the candidate to reflect on their practice, for example, by asking, 'What might you do differently next time?', 'What did you learn from that?'
- Use positive body language, for example, smiling and nodding your head, to show that you are interested in the candidate's response.

Over to you!
Questioning candidates

Imagine that you have observed a candidate feeding a baby a bottle, towards *Unit 314*. What questions might you ask the candidate at the end of the observation to check their knowledge and understanding of the actions they have performed?

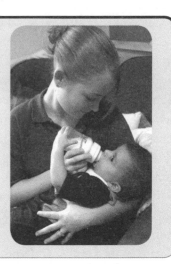

Witness testimonies

> **Witness testimony**
>
> An account of a candidate's performance, written by someone other than the candidate's assessor

Witness testimonies are written by witnesses who were present at a particular time, and can confirm consistency of the candidate's practice, but are not expert witnesses (see following page). Practitioners who write witness testimonies must only write what they have witnessed, and the testimony must be written by the witness themselves. In the past, it may have been accepted for the candidate to write the testimony and ask the witness to sign it; however, this does not demonstrate validity or authenticity and therefore should not be accepted as evidence.

Some training centres have their own format for writing witness testimonies, and will supply witnesses with printed sheets to write their testimony on. Alternatively, a testimony on a piece of headed paper will be fine, as long as it is signed and dated appropriately. If witness testimonies are used within the portfolio as evidence, the candidate must also provide a witness status list. A witness status list identifies the name, status and signature of anyone involved within the candidate's portfolio, such as a teacher who writes a witness statement, or an expert witness. A pro-forma of this can be found within your standards, and should state clearly the name and status of the witness, along with their signature. It is also good practice to clarify the authenticity of a random selection of witness testimonies as part of your centre's quality assurance procedures.

Again, witness testimonies can be useful for units that are particularly difficult to directly observe or where the candidate has shown competence at a time when you were not there.

An example of this might be on an outing with the children. For example, the candidate might have supported an ill child, responded to an emergency or worked particularly well as part of the team. In such a case, a witness could write a testimony to prove competence within this area.

Over to you!
Witness testimonies

Read the following witness testimony, written by the manager of a private day nursery and consider how you might reference it to the Level 2 NOS.

Name: Lisa Morris   **Status:** Nursery Manager

Date: 11th October 2005

'AJ was working with a small group of 2-3-year-olds, when the fire alarm began to sound. I had not informed any of the staff that I was going to have a practice, so they considered it to be an actual emergency. AJ calmly gathered her children together, explaining to them what was happening, and asked them to "line up like we do when we have a practice". She followed all policies and procedures of the nursery, and acted in a professional manner, escorting the children to our playground, which is the designated meeting point. She assisted me to call the register, and comforted a new child, who had got a little upset. AJ then wrote the outcomes of the drill in the record book, and sent a memo to all staff outlining the areas for improvement. She also informed parents of the drill as they collected their children.'

Signed: *L Morris*

Expert witness evidence

This type of evidence is very similar to direct observation; however, it is written by the expert witness, not you. **Expert witness** evidence is used primarily where there are no occupationally competent assessors for occupationally specific units. Expert witnesses are employed within the candidate's setting and must be approved and trained by the training centre. Records of expert witnesses must be kept up to date. Expert witness evidence is extremely valuable for providing evidence on confidential matters, where your presence could

Expert witness

An approved practitioner, inducted by the training centre, who carries out observations on the candidate in order to provide written evidence.

be inappropriate. The CCLD assessment strategy states that expert witnesses must demonstrate:

- a working knowledge of the relevant NOS
- current or recent (within the last two years) experience of working at or above the level for which they are attesting competence
- appropriate, continuous professional development relevant to the sector for which they are attesting competence
- no conflict of interest in the outcome of their evidence.

It is not necessary for expert witnesses to hold an assessor qualification, as a qualified assessor must assess the contribution of performance evidence drawn from an expert witness to overall evidence of competence.

Over to you!
Expert witnesses

Consider the kind of information you might keep on file regarding individual expert witnesses.

Case studies, projects and assignments

Used to provide evidence where no naturally occurring evidence is available.

Case studies, projects and assignments

Previously, this type of evidence has been relied on too heavily, with candidates producing masses of written evidence. The S/NVQ process is all about real work evidence and candidates should not be producing written evidence for each unit of the NOS. This type of evidence should be used where there is no naturally occurring evidence available or where knowledge evidence cannot be observed. For example, your candidate might demonstrate competence working with children within a particular age range through direct observation, but use case studies, projects or assignments to demonstrate their knowledge of other age ranges.

Over to you!
Written evidence

Imagine that you have a candidate working in a playscheme with 7–11-year-olds. They have no prior experience of working with children. What project could you set them to demonstrate the *Knowledge Specification K3D217* within *Unit 303*?

Reflective accounts

Reflective accounts are written by the candidates themselves, and should be detailed accounts of their practice. These accounts should give candidates the opportunity to think through their practice, consider their progression and identify future development needs. Candidates should be encouraged to reflect on their practice, and include this reflection within their account, identifying how their practice has improved as a result. Your candidates can also provide reflective accounts orally to you, which you could record on audio tape, in writing or on video tape. Your training centre may have its own format for recording reflective accounts. It is important that these are not too prescriptive, but allow the candidates to write their accounts in their own way.

> **Reflective account**
> A written or oral account by the candidate reflecting on their practice.

Reflective accounts should demonstrate:

- what went well
- what could have gone better
- what could have been done differently
- the candidate's role
- what the candidate has learnt
- what can be done to improve the candidate's performance and practice.

Over to you!
Reflective accounts

Read through this reflective account. Consider what advice you would give the candidate to improve future reflective accounts.

Name: Dave Harrison

Date: 3rd April 2006

Setting: Lonsdale After School Club

Today we had a total of 13 children in the Club, ranging from 5–9 years of age. I was scheduled to supervise outdoor play activities. I asked the children what they would like to do and they wanted to play rounders. I set up the rounders pitch and explained the rules to the children. I chose two team captains, and the captains chose their team players. We then started to play. After a while, one child began to cry because they had been caught out. I explained that they shouldn't be upset because it is taking part that counts. All the players agreed to let the child continue playing, as they were only interested in playing, not which team wins. I supervised the game, making sure that they all played fairly, and encouraged them when they were playing. I think that the game went well, and we carried on playing until it was time to go inside for a drink.

Work products

Throughout the duration of the course, your candidate may produce work products, both from their working practice and their training sessions. These could be minutes from meetings, leaflets, child observation, curriculum plans, and so on. It is important that your candidates realise that, while these products are worthwhile to their learning and as reference material, they may not be necessary as evidence within their portfolios. You might suggest to your candidates that they have a 'working file' in which to keep all of this supplementary evidence. Should any of these products become required for evidence, they can then be put into the portfolio or, better still, referenced into the NOS and kept in the working file. Candidates should not include photographs or any personal details of children. Candidates should also be aware that work products must have been produced by them, and not someone else within the setting.

Simulation

> **Simulation**
>
> Setting up an observation that is not within a real work situation. Only to be used where clearly indicated within the NOS.

This type of evidence should only be used as directed by the NOS. **Simulation** can only be used if no other evidence is available and only where it is stated within the NOS. Where there is no alternative, you must endeavour to make the simulation as realistic as possible, and the candidate must demonstrate their competency in the same manner as they would in a real work situation, including following all policies and procedures of their setting. Simulation may never be the sole source of evidence within an element.

An example of this could be sterilisation of bottles for a baby. The candidate may demonstrate competence via direct observation for the method used within the placement, but then use simulation to try out other methods, and prove competence.

Accreditation of prior learning

This evidence type can be used when candidates have prior learning experiences that have been certificated. For example, your candidates might have been on a first aid course or behaviour management course, and you could therefore reference this evidence accordingly. Your centre should have an **Accreditation of Prior Learning (APL)** policy, outlining how APL should be carried out. You will need to see original copies of certificates, and can put copies of these certificates in the portfolio, although this isn't necessary as you can write an observation of the product. You may want to clarify the knowledge the candidate has actually got from this APL during a professional discussion. The stages to APL are as follows.

1 Identify what the candidate can do or has learnt.
2 Identify how those skills and knowledge relate to the CCLD NOS.
3 Reference accordingly.

> **Accreditation of Prior Learning (APL)**
> Identifying candidates' previous learning experiences and referencing them accordingly to the NOS.

Planning for effective assessment opportunities

As you have seen, there is a range of possible assessment opportunities available to your candidate, in order for them to demonstrate their competence, skills, knowledge and understanding. To ensure that the candidate uses these opportunities effectively, the assessments must be planned and scheduled, detailing how the assessments will support and enhance the achievement of the award.

Forward planning is instrumental in our daily lives. From planning holidays and trips to managing day-to-day tasks, we all need to plan in order to effectively achieve our goals and ambitions. The same planning principles you use personally can be put into practice when supporting your candidates' learning and assessment opportunities.

It is important that your candidates take responsibility for their own planning and learning from the beginning of their training, understanding how to make the most of the assessment opportunities available to them. Planning assessments will ensure that candidates are aware of their goals and targets, which in turn will help them to achieve their qualification and plan any further training they might want to undertake. Planning will provide your candidates with a clear sense of direction and enable them to assess their own progress.

Careful planning will also help you to meet the individual needs of your candidates, and understand how best to support them through their training. There are many methods for planning, and a good assessor will use a combination of planning methods, being led by the individual needs of their candidates.

Arranging assessment opportunities is central to the success of S/NVQ training, and will:

- help identify the opportunities for collecting evidence efficiently across a range of elements
- ensure that the evidence collected is authentic, valid and reliable
- encourage candidates to take ownership of their learning and assessment
- help candidates see how their work practice relates to the NOS
- help to avoid the collection of too much evidence.

Where to start

Before planning any assessments with a candidate, you must first find out about their goals, ambitions, previous experiences and abilities. You could ask your candidate the following questions and find out the following information.

- What do you want to achieve?
- What were the results of the initial assessment and diagnostic screening?
- What prior achievements and experiences have you already had, and do these link into the CCLD NOS?
- How might your previous learning experiences affect your training now?
- What options do you have available to you – e.g. placements, training, workshops, etc.?
- What support do you feel you require?

All of the information gathered during this initial discussion will allow you to build a picture of the candidate's starting point and begin to plan how you will support them in achieving their award. This information should be agreed and recorded within their **Individual Learning Plan (ILP)**.

Individual Learning Plans

You will almost certainly find that your training centre has an ILP for each candidate. The ILP has many uses, not only for the assessor, but the candidate, internal verifier and training centre.

ILPs can inform the assessment and learning process for all concerned, providing a systematic tool for the development

---

Individual Learning Plan (ILP)

A flexible tool that is used by the assessor to assess candidates' accomplishments and/ or needs in essential knowledge, skills and abilities.

of learning, and offering a way to record the advice, support and guidance given to candidates at appropriate intervals. An ILP should be used as a working document, which is referred to throughout the learning process, measuring the candidate's progress and setting clear targets for achievement, and subsequently reviewing the progress of these targets or goals. The ILP could also identify previous achievements that your candidate has made, and provide you with an insight into the candidate's prior experiences of learning. You would then use this information when planning assessments with that candidate. All the information gathered from the **initial assessment** and **diagnostic screening** will be noted within the ILP as an integral part of the learning process, providing a platform from which to begin planning.

The purposes and uses of the ILP may be to:

- ensure that assessment is focused on the needs of the individual candidate
- set measurable goals so that achievement of candidates can be assessed
- specify learning goals and targets that can be measured and assessed
- provide candidates with a sense of direction, and a focus
- provide a tool for motivation as candidates see their training progressing.

Initial assessment and diagnostic screening enable you to fully understand and identify the levels and abilities of your candidate, allowing you to ensure they are signposted to the appropriate course and/or level of training. The diagnostic assessment will allow more detailed information on the skills of the candidate, for example, in literacy or numeracy. Candidates should not feel as if this screening is an exam or test, but should be made aware that it is a tool to ensure the best possible learning outcomes for them. Initial assessment and diagnostic screening may identify particular support needs that you need to consider during their training on the CCLD, such as language, literacy or numeracy support. The results of initial assessment and diagnostic screening will assist both you and your candidates to identify a starting point and develop an ILP.

Initial assessment

Assesses starting levels and identifies appropriate learning opportunities.

Diagnostic screening

Identifies skills and weaknesses to inform the Individual Learning Plan (ILP).

Check it out

You can find out more about initial assessment and diagnostic screening at www.basic-skills.co.uk

Planning and setting goals and targets

When planning assessment opportunities and setting goals and targets with your candidate, you must also negotiate a timescale for achievement of these goals. You might start by carrying out a holistic assessment (see page 59) within the setting, whereby only the time and place is planned. Candidates who have never experienced direct observation before can find the idea of their first observation very daunting. If the first holistic observation is to observe the candidate's general work situation, the candidate will not feel the pressure to 'perform'.

You should discuss with your candidate the shift patterns they will be working, the ages of the children they will be working with, and agree a date and time for the observation to take place. It is important to reassure the candidate that they should be relaxed and carry out their duties as they normally would. This first observation will allow you to get a feel for the setting, the candidate and the candidate's responsibilities.

After this observation, you might want to cross-reference the evidence in the candidate's portfolio while explaining to the candidate the elements and units they have provided evidence for. This will demonstrate how their work practice meets the requirements of the NOS and can be very motivating to candidates as they see their portfolio being referenced.

Once this first observation has been carried out, you can begin to set goals and targets for completion. It is a good idea to set smaller targets within larger goals. This will make the goals more achievable and will act as a motivational tool for the candidate. It is important that you agree with the candidate how the success of each target will be measured. For example, you may agree a goal of completing *Unit 202 Help to keep children safe*. Within this goal you would negotiate smaller targets for completion and how the success of these would be developed. An assessment plan for *Unit 202* might look something like the assessment plan reproduced on page 77.

Upon completion of each assessment, it is necessary to review the progress of the candidate and, if necessary, review the set goals and targets. The review should allow the candidate to reflect on their practice and consider how they might improve their knowledge or practice in the future. During the review, you should discuss with your candidate how they are

Over to you!
Planning assessment opportunities

Imagine you were planning assessment opportunities with a candidate, with an emphasis on completing *Unit 206*. Copy and complete the assessment plan below, detailing the types of assessment opportunity the candidate could use to demonstrate their competence, knowledge and understanding for this unit.

Assessment Plan

Award: .... Date: ....

Candidate's Name: .... Candidate PIN No: ....

Assessor's Name: ....

Evidence to be gathered	Date	By whom	Achieved

progressing, by ensuring they understand how their evidence is relating to the NOS, so demonstrating their competence and abilities.

A final or exit review should always take place when the candidate has achieved their award. This allows them to consider their further options, review their overall achievements and ask for further support and guidance. This will provide you with an opportunity to ensure that the candidate has a career/training plan in mind. You might also like to signpost them to further training or employment opportunities.

Judging evidence and providing feedback

Judging evidence

Making judgements on evidence is fairly straightforward, providing you apply all the principles of assessment and evidence collection to all the evidence provided, and are guided by the NOS and the S/NVQ Code of Practice. So what are the principles for producing and judging S/NVQ assessment?

- **Authenticity:** You should be sure that the evidence is authentic and that it belongs to and has been solely generated by the candidate themselves.
- **Consistency:** The candidate needs to demonstrate that their performance is consistent over a period of time.
- **Currency:** The evidence must demonstrate that it is relevant to today's standards of practice and reflects current legislative requirements and policy for practice.
- **Realistic:** The candidate's evidence must have been generated under real work conditions.
- **Reliability:** You should ensure that the evidence accurately reflects the level of performance that has been demonstrated by the candidate.
- **Sufficiency:** You need to be sure that the evidence is enough to demonstrate that all Performance Criteria and knowledge evidence requirements have been met.
- **Validity:** The evidence must have been gathered using appropriate and required assessment methods, that are relevant to the standards for which competence is being claimed.

Using the above principles will allow you to ensure that the evidence submitted for internal verification meets the requirements of the standards, and that you are confident in the abilities, skills, knowledge and understanding of your candidates.

Providing feedback

Providing feedback to your candidates on their performance and your assessment decision requires skill and forethought. Constructive feedback can:

- support ongoing learning and development
- support candidates in their ongoing personal and professional development
- increase self-awareness and reflection
- encourage a positive workplace and training environment.

Keys to good practice
Giving feedback

- **Be descriptive not evaluative**

  For example, say, 'I noticed you forgot to complete the incident book . . .' instead of, 'You didn't complete the incident book. . . .' By feeding back in this way, your candidate will not respond in a defensive manner.

- **Keep your feedback specific**

  Focus on actual specific events, rather than generalising, for example, 'I liked the way you dealt with the parents' enquiry about the menu' is much better than, 'I find you work well with parents.'

- **Focus on the behaviour, not on the person**

  Always discuss the behaviour or what the candidate has done. An example of this might be, 'I notice you find it a little difficult to put your ideas across in training sessions' rather than, 'You lack confidence.'

- **Be aware of the needs and feelings of the candidate**

  Always take into account the needs and feelings of the candidate, for example, 'I would have liked to have seen you converse a little more during that art activity with the children' not, 'That was a pointless activity, why didn't you chat with the children?'

- **Always feed back on something that can be changed or improved**

  Giving feedback to a candidate on something that they cannot improve is counter-productive and frustrating for the candidate.

- **Consider the time and place**

  Always feed back as soon after the assessment as possible. This ensures that the assessment is still fresh in your mind and the candidate's. Feedback will also be more effective if it is given in a supportive and friendly environment.

- **Share good practice**

  Your feedback should provide the candidate with an opportunity to reflect on their practice and to decide for themselves whether or not to act on the information and advice you are giving them. For example, 'Sarah had found a great website full of information about that, why don't you have a chat with her?' is better than, 'You will need to research that information.'

- **Consider how much feedback to give**

  Overloading your candidate with feedback means that they may not take it all on board. Making notes with constructive action points will help the candidate to remember what has been discussed and to make future improvements.

- **Think about it**

  Always consider what feedback you want to give the candidate, and how you will advise them.

The manner in which you feed back to your candidate needs to enhance, not damage their confidence and self-esteem. When giving feedback, it is important to help your candidates keep things in perspective and understand that they have not failed. Ideally, you should discuss your decisions with the candidate at the end of each assessment, allowing them time to reflect on their practice and discuss with you how they can improve on their practice in the future. Feedback should be an opportunity for identifying strengths and areas for development, and considering how this development might take place. For example, you might have a candidate who has a positive manner with the children, and who works hard, fitting in with the team. You might, however, identify during an observation that she has difficulty communicating with parents. The feedback at the end of the observation will provide you with an opportunity to discuss this with her, informing her of how well she works with the children and the team, and offering suggestions as to how she could implement these skills when working with parents. You could suggest, for example, that she attend a particular workshop or read a specific article. Whatever the feedback, it needs to be constructive and you should identify a way of measuring the success of the actions suggested to the candidate.

Keys to good practice
Giving constructive feedback

- Choose the right time.
- Start with positive comments.
- Encourage self-assessment.
- Draw attention to and reinforce strengths, as well as areas for improvement.
- Ask questions rather than making statements.
- Be specific, giving explicit examples.
- Refer to behaviour that can be changed.
- Demonstrate what should and could be done to improve.
- Set deadlines and targets for improvement.
- Be descriptive rather than evaluative.
- Ensure the candidate fully understands what is being discussed.

E-portfolios

The idea of a portfolio is to collect and manage assessment evidence within the S/NVQ process. E-portfolios do the same job, except they are electronic versions as opposed to paper-based ones, holding the evidence electronically.

E-portfolios are becoming increasingly popular within centres, as they strive to provide high-class training and keep up to date with modern technology. They allow flexibility for the candidates, as they can access the portfolios at any time, as well as enabling them to contact their assessor and view their own progress. Table 3 identifies the advantages that some of the e-portfolio systems on the market offer.

Table 3 Advantages of e-portfolios

	Advantages
Candidate	• Identifies to the candidate what needs to be done in order to proceed to the next stage of the assessment process. • The candidate can send a message to their assessor for further assistance. • The candidate has the opportunity to be proactive in the assessment process. • Instant charts, diagrams and reports can show the candidate exactly how far they have progressed in their units. • Candidates are motivated by the easy-to-use and stimulating point-and-click interface. • There is no need to carry a large and heavy portfolio around. • The portfolio can be viewed over the internet from any number of locations at any time of day. • The portfolio can be worked on at the same time by both candidate and assessor, even without their being in the same room. • More diverse assessment methods, such as sound files, digital photos or video recordings, can be used.
Assessor	• Helps with assessing criteria-based qualifications, such as S/NVQs, Key Skills and Basic Skills. • Time-saving benefits include cross-referencing and instant progress reporting. • Both the candidate and the assessor are able to access the portfolio simultaneously. • Hard copies of written work completed offline can be scanned and uploaded as an image attachment, as can other media files, such as audio and visual files. • There is less to carry around and less storage is required. • Enforces a training centre's assessment consistency by implementing customised rules and procedures.
Internal verifier	• Internal verifiers are sent a task to complete as soon as a unit has been signed off by an assessor. • The unit or the entire portfolio can be verified remotely, meaning a faster verification and feedback time to the assessor. • Assessors are peripatetic so there is no travel time wasted in picking up or dropping off portfolios. • A database automatically generates a matrix of anticipated completion dates set against candidates and the units they are studying, from which the verifier can set their sampling plan without having to wait for information from the centre or the assessor. • A verifier can access any page of a candidate's portfolio directly, using hyperlinks, without having to search through a paper-based portfolio or struggle with plastic wallets.

	Advantages
Centre	• Systems can be used to assess any criteria-based qualification, such as S/NVQs, Key Skills, Basic Skills and Technical Certificates. • Assessment units can be individually standardised for consistency and any assessment methods. • A detailed audit trail is provided to track candidate, assessor and verifier productivity. • Built-in security ensures that each user login only has access to the pages and processes that should be available to them. • A wide range of reports on the different aspects of the assessment process can be run out, such as candidate progress, visits made by assessors, placement efficiency and time spent logged in. • There is no paperwork involved and no storage is required for portfolios. • Savings should be made in many areas, such as manpower, purchase of portfolios, paper, photocopying, postage and petrol. • With increased motivation, the candidates should progress quicker and therefore finish sooner, which will mean higher achievement rates and higher retention rates as, with a quicker completion time, there will be less opportunity for candidates to leave.

Case study OneFile

OneFile is a portfolio assessment solution for training companies to deliver their courses over the internet. OneFile can be used as a wholly remote assessment tool or in conjunction with face-to-face visits between a candidate and an assessor. Courses can include National/Scottish Vocational Qualifications (NVQ/SVQ), Key Skills, Basic Skills and other performance-criteria-based assessments.

OneFile provides a secure online portfolio, accessible via the internet, 24 hours a day, 7 days a week. Everyone who uses OneFile has a unique login that gives them different levels of access to a candidate's portfolio depending on their role in the assessment process. OneFile supports candidates, assessors, verifiers (internal and external), managers and monitors. The system also supports those unqualified assessors and verifiers, and implements, for example, the role of a second-line assessor.

OneFile overcomes the problems found with traditional paper-based systems by improving efficiency between the people involved in the assessment process. For example, an assessor can set and provide feedback to assessments between visits without the need for face-to-face contact. At the same time, verifiers can also access the portfolios from different locations without the portfolio being taken away from the candidate and assessor.

For the training centre manager, OneFile provides a comprehensive and detailed management reporting and auditing system. At the touch of a button, managers can track candidate progress, candidate and assessor productivity, detailed activity logs, and much more, without having to rely on the assessor for the information required. There is a full audit trail of the assessment processes and methods used, including cancellations of visits and pastoral reviews that may be required for contractual purposes, including times and dates.

For more information on the OneFile system visit www.onefile.co.uk.

Check your understanding

As you have reached the end of this chapter, you may find it useful to consolidate all that you have learnt by answering the following questions. You will find suggested answers in the back of the book on page 179.

1 List three main assessment opportunities.
2 What information about an expert witness would you keep on file?
3 List five things that you would consider when giving feedback.
4 What questions could you ask to encourage a candidate to reflect on their practice?
5 Why would you use questioning as an assessment opportunity?
6 Who would write a witness testimony?
7 Why is it important to plan assessment opportunities in advance?
8 List three purposes of the Individual Learning Plan (ILP).
9 What is the difference between initial assessment and diagnostic screening?

Chapter 4

The A1 and A2 awards

Introduction

Working as an assessor involves commitment to your own personal training and development, as well as that of your candidate. This chapter looks at the requirements of the A1 and A2 qualifications, and the importance of keeping your competence up to date. This chapter will guide you through the A1 award, detailing how you can generate evidence to prove your competence and ultimately gain your qualification.

You will look at who is involved in the S/NVQ assessment process and what their job roles and responsibilities are. The final section of this chapter addresses the requirements of quality and standardisation across all S/NVQ awards.

This chapter will help you to understand:
- the structure of the A1 and A2 awards
- who is who
- quality assurance and standardisation.

Check it out

Throughout this chapter, references will be made to specific pieces of legislation, and you will find it useful to obtain a copy of and make yourself familiar with the following documents.

- *Joint Awarding Body Guidance for S/NVQs and VQs in Children's Care, Learning and Development*, which is available from QCA at www.qca.org.uk
- The A1 NOS, which you can get from your awarding body

Check it out

Find out more about the work of ENTO at www.ento.org.uk

The structure of the A1 and A2 awards

To be able to practise as a fully qualified assessor, you must work towards the A1 or A2 award and gain appropriate knowledge and experience in the assessment of S/NVQs. Until recently, the awards were taken from the National Occupational Standards in Training and Development, and were called D32/33. In 2002, the S/NVQs in Training and Development were replaced by the S/NVQs in Learning and Development, and the Employment National Training Organisation (ENTO) carried out a review of the old D-units, bringing them into line with current practice.

Table 1 demonstrates the changes that have taken place:

Table 1 Changes from old D-units to A1/A2 awards

New unit number	New title	Old unit
A1	Assess candidates using a range of methods	D32+33
A2	Assess candidates' performance through observation	D32
V1	Conduct internal quality assurance of the assessment process	D34
V2	Conduct external quality assurance of the assessment process	D35

While using the previous awards, it was recognised that most assessors were completing two of the D-units (D32 and D33) and that, by doing so, assessors were actually overlapping the skills and requirements for the awards. In response to this, the A1 award combines both the old D32 and D33 units, and so satisfies the requirements of the majority of assessors. However, there may be some specialist assessors within some sectors or industries who only assess candidates by observation. In such cases, they may prefer to take the A2 award instead. The following case study shows an example of this.

The V1 and V2 awards are concerned with verification of S/NVQ awards. V1 is for those wishing to become internal verifiers, working specifically for centres, whereas V2 is for those wishing to become external verifiers, working for awarding bodies. You can find out more about these roles later in this chapter (see pages 107–108).

Case study Cheeky's Playgroup

Cheeky's Playgroup is in a small rural village, catering for up to 30 sessional children. Sarah McKay, manager, explains why she chose the A2 award.

'I was approached by two young people who wanted to use the playgroup as their work placement during their training and we were more than happy to have them. The students were very good, and although their assessors visited them regularly, I felt that the assessor often missed seeing their good practice throughout the day. I was looking at developing my skills and decided to take the A2 award. I don't want to be an assessor and didn't want to do the whole A1, so the A2 seemed to be the right choice. The A2 has allowed me to assess the students who use us as a placement, therefore ensuring their good practice is not missed. When something unplanned happens, such as a fire drill or first aid incident, I can see it first-hand, whereas the assessor finds it difficult to assess such naturally occurring evidence. I write the observations as I see them, and the college assessor references them in the student's portfolio. The students achieve their qualifications in a faster time, as I see everything holistically, and can observe it there and then. The college arranged for my training, and I attend regular standardisation meetings with them to ensure that I keep myself up to date with current guidance.'

The A units also form part of other qualifications within the Learning and Development suite of awards. As your training and assessing role develops, you may wish to work towards further awards, such as those listed in Table 2.

Check it out

Find out more about further Learning and Development awards at www.ento.org.uk

Table 2 Further awards to work towards

Qualification
Level 3 Learning and Development
Level 3 Advice and Guidance
Level 4 Management of Learning and Development Provision
Level 4 Co-ordination of Learning and Development Provision

A1 Certificate in assessing candidates using a range of methods

This unit is designed for individuals who assess candidates against the National Occupational Standards (NOS) using a range of assessment methods. The evidence you present in your portfolio will demonstrate your ability to develop assessment plans with your candidates, based on their individual needs and the requirements of the NOS. You will demonstrate how you judge the evidence presented to you by your candidates against the NOS, indicating the outcome or decision you have made. You will also need to demonstrate the assessment methods you use, and why you have chosen these assessment methods for particular candidates. This unit demands that you provide feedback to your candidates, informing them of your assessment decisions and explaining how you came to those decisions, as well as how they can move forward in their learning. You will also need to demonstrate how you contribute to the internal verification processes and quality assurance.

Over to you!
Using a range of assessment methods

Consider what is meant by the term 'using a range of assessment methods'. What assessment methods do you think you will be using with your candidates and how will you provide evidence for your A1 award?

It is important to remember that the award is assessed on actual work-based performance, so you will need to demonstrate your ability to perform the roles of the job as

well as presenting products of assessment, such as assessment plans. Your assessor will directly observe you carrying out direct observations on your candidates in order to demonstrate your skills and abilities.

Your assessor will work with you to devise an action plan, just as you would with your CCLD candidates. This will demonstrate how you will work towards achieving your A1 award. The action plan will note the types of activity you may be carrying out.

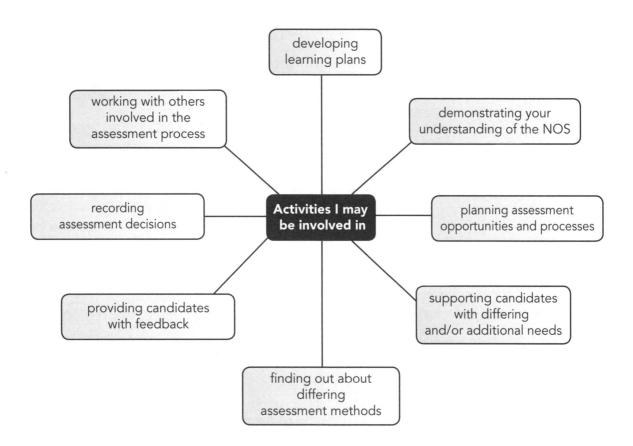

Your action plan may look something like this:

A1 Award Action Plan

Name <u>Chris James</u>   **PIN No** <u>05/478573</u>

Date	Unit / Element	Current evidence available	Further evidence required	Action	By when	Completion date
24th May 2005	A1.2: Judge evidence against criteria to make assessment decisions	Assessment decision from reflective account written by candidate (a)	• Two further assessment decisions • Professional discussion	CJ to work with candidates to produce two further assessment decisions. Professional discussion to be carried out	14th June 2005	

The A1 unit is broken down into four elements:

A1.1 Develop plans for assessing competence with candidates

A1.2 Judge evidence against criteria to make assessment decisions

A1.3 Provide feedback and support to candidates on assessment decisions

A1.4 Contribute to the internal quality assurance processes.

As with the CCLD NOS, the A1 award carries knowledge requirements that you must meet. The table below shows each knowledge requirement, and identifies what they are looking for.

Table 3   A1 knowledge requirements

Knowledge requirement	What does this mean and how might this be demonstrated?

A record of a professional discussion between the assessor and the assessor-candidate during which the assessor reviews any method of the assessment not covered by performance evidence and:
 	
• indicates the validity and reliability of each method
• reviews any potential issues of fairness and access in relation to individual assessment methods
• covers all of the following methods if not covered by performance evidence:
  • questioning
  • accreditation of prior experience and achievement
  • formal testing
  • projects and assignments
  • simulations
  • candidates' and peer reports
  • evidence from others.
	Your assessor will carry out a professional discussion with you, focusing particularly on any assessment methods that you have not demonstrated during your performance with your candidate. Your assessor will need you to discuss how various assessment methods provide reliable and valuable evidence, and indicate how this may be compromised if the assessment is not carried out fairly. They may question your choice of assessment method for a particular candidate, and you will need to justify your choices for this decision. The professional discussion will ensure that all assessment methods are discussed, and that you have an in-depth knowledge of the assessment process and of how to meet the needs of your individual candidates. Questions your assessor might ask during the professional discussion include the following.
	
	• How might you check the validity of a witness statement?
	• Why is it important to plan professional discussions?
	• What factors would you consider when asking verbal questions of your candidate?
	• How do you consider the individual needs of your candidates?

Knowledge requirement	What does this mean and how might this be demonstrated?
A written or spoken explanation of the following procedures used within the assessor-candidate's centre. • How to provide access to assessment for candidates with individual special needs and special assessment requirements • How disputes and appeals about assessment decisions are handled • The internal standardisation and quality assurance arrangements • How assessments are recorded • Sources of information regarding assessment requirements and best practice.	This written or spoken explanation will allow you to demonstrate your knowledge of your centre's policies and procedures and show your understanding of best practice. You will need to provide examples of access to assessment, and may do this by showing your assessor assessment plans that you have written for a candidate with particular needs. Your assessor will encourage you to think about how you maintain the confidentiality of your candidates and the strategies you use to empower them. If you have handled a complaint or dispute, the paperwork for this will be a good source of evidence to demonstrate your skills and knowledge in this area. You should also show your assessor any minutes from standardisation meetings or comments from your internal verifier regarding your work. The discussion will allow you to show your understanding of the assessment strategy and of anti-discriminatory practice.

A1.1 Develop plans for assessing competence with candidates

This element requires you to demonstrate your knowledge and skills when planning assessment opportunities with your candidates. You will need to show your assessor that you can assist your candidates in forward planning their learning, and support them in taking ownership of their development. Assessment planning will help to ensure that your candidates are aware of their learning and assessment opportunities, and provide them with a clear sense of direction. Careful planning will also help you to meet the individual needs of your candidates and understand how best to support them through their training. Assessment plans should show how your candidate will:

• identify the opportunities for collecting evidence across a range of elements
• ensure that their evidence is authentic, valid, safe and reliable

- take ownership of their learning and assessment
- relate their work practice to the NOS
- avoid the collection of too much evidence.

Your A1 NOS will show the Performance Criteria and knowledge evidence you will need to cover, and will specify the amount and type of evidence that you will need to provide to show you have met the requirements of this element.

Over to you!
A1.1 Develop plans for assessing competence with candidates

Using your A1 NOS, identify the evidence requirements for element A1.1.

1 _____

_____

2 _____

_____

3 _____

_____

Assessment plans

The A1 NOS require that each assessment plan covers one full unit of competence that can be certificated. This means that you need to demonstrate how you have planned with your candidates how they will achieve a full unit. These plans must clearly specify which assessment methods will be used and how the assessment will take place. The assessment methods used will be entirely based upon the needs of the candidate and the requirements of the unit they are working towards; however, you must cover a minimum of four assessment methods, one of which must be observation of the candidate's work practice. You must also provide an example of how others have made a contribution to the assessment process, such as through a witness statement. It is essential that all paperwork, particularly assessments and plans, are signed and dated, in order to provide a clear audit trail of validity.

Over to you!
Assessment plans

Jackie is a Level 3 student who has been undertaking CCLD Level 3 for about six months. You are her assessor and the evidence you generate with Jackie will be used as evidence within your A1 portfolio. Jackie is employed as an assistant at a private day nursery where she works full-time in the baby room alongside another practitioner with six under-ones. Copy and complete the assessment plan below to demonstrate how Jackie will generate the evidence to complete *Unit 302 Develop and maintain a healthy, safe and secure environment for children.*

Assessment Plan

Award: CCLD L3   **Date:** 14ᵗʰ September 2005

Candidate's Name: Jackie Simpson   **Candidate PIN No:** 05/245363

Assessor's Name: T. Assessor   **Unit/Element:** 302

Evidence	Element reference	Knowledge specification reference	By whom	By when

Record of written or spoken explanation

This is an opportunity for you to discuss your assessment plans with your assessor, indicating why you have made your decisions. Your assessor may tape the discussion, and it should be kept pretty informal. It is an opportunity for you to demonstrate why you chose the particular assessment methods and how you feel they will assess specific aspects of your candidate's competence. You should draw on your knowledge of your candidate's preferred learning style and explain how you have considered their individual needs. You should also discuss how the methods you have chosen are valid, reliable and fair, and cover the minimum four assessment methods. During this explanation, you should identify how others have been involved in the process and how their contributions will benefit the overall assessment of your candidate's competence. The plans will demonstrate what assessment methods you want your candidate to use and the discussion allows you to explain why you have made those decisions.

Written outcomes from progress reviews

In order to cover this evidence requirement you need to carry out progress reviews with a minimum of two candidates, demonstrating how you have updated assessment plans in response to the progress review. Chapter 3 looked at the review process (see pages 57–85), which is necessary to review the progress of the candidate and, if required, review the set goals and targets. This progress review provides the candidate with the opportunity to reflect on their practice, and consider how they might improve their knowledge or practice in the future. The review allows you to discuss with your candidate how they are progressing and ensure they understand how their evidence is relating to the NOS, so demonstrating their competence and abilities.

A1.2 Judge evidence against criteria to make assessment decisions

> **Over to you!**
>
> ### A1.2 Judge evidence against criteria to make assessment decisions
>
> Using your A1 NOS, identify the evidence requirements for element A1.2.
>
> 1 _____
>
> _____
>
> 2 _____
>
> _____

Assessment decision records

Assessment decision records must be for a minimum of two different candidates and relate directly to the three assessment plans you generated for A1.1.

> **Over to you!**
>
> ### Assessment decision records
>
> Look back at the assessment plan on page 95. Consider how you will generate assessment decision records that relate directly to this plan.

The professional discussion

This discussion is between you and your assessor, and provides you with an opportunity to indicate how you have used three different types of evidence to demonstrate your candidate's achievement towards the CCLD NOS, ensuring you use direct observation as one of these methods. You will explain how you carried out the assessments, and be able to evaluate how effective these assessment methods were in meeting the requirements of the NOS. You will also be required to demonstrate to your assessor how you ensured that the evidence was fair, safe, valid and reliable, and how your overall assessment decision was based on the candidate's performance and knowledge.

A1.3 Provide feedback and support to candidates on assessment decisions

For this element, you are required to demonstrate your ability to provide constructive feedback at an appropriate time and place to your candidates, ensuring that they understand your assessment decision and agree the next steps for achievement. The evidence requirements for A1.3 are:

- a minimum of one observation
- a record of a professional discussion.

The observation

This is when your assessor will observe you providing feedback to your candidate. Your assessor will remain unobtrusive throughout the observation, and you should prepare your candidate, letting them know that you are being observed, but that they have nothing to worry about. Sometimes this can make candidates feel on edge, and therefore you should consider the appropriateness of this for your candidates, along with any confidentiality issues. For example, you might be aware of particular concerns your candidate is having, and should consider the appropriateness of having a third party present within the feedback session. For this reason, you should choose your observational candidates wisely. This observation of feedback should also be supported by evidence of feedback being given on two other occasions, ideally in the form of copies of feedback previously given to candidates.

Over to you!
The observation

Look back again at Chapter 3 at the section *Providing feedback* (page 78). Consider how your practice ensures that the feedback given is constructive and encouraging. Think about a time when you received negative feedback, and consider the implications of this and how you felt at that time.

That seemed a bit of a pointless activity. It didn't look as if they were having much fun.

Record of a professional discussion

Again, this professional discussion will be between you and your assessor, and may link with the discussion for A1.2. This discussion will focus on providing feedback to your candidates, and identify the following points.

- Was the feedback given to the candidate at an appropriate place and time?
- Was the candidate given advice on how to prove their competence and how to develop the necessary skills or provide further evidence?
- Were you able to identify and agree the next steps in the assessment process and how they will be achieved?

A1.4 Contribute to the internal quality assurance process

This final element of the award requires you to demonstrate how you maintain the accuracy of assessment records, and provide an audit trail of evidence. You will need to show your assessor evidence of attendance at standardisation meetings, and give accurate and timely information on assessments. The evidence requirements for A1.4 are:

- one assessment record each for two different candidates, which must have been used as part of the internal quality assurance process
- the review of at least two pieces of evidence for each of two different candidates which must have contributed to internal standardisation procedures
- a written statement from the person responsible for the internal quality assurance, showing that you have contributed to agreed quality assurance procedures.

The submission of evidence for this unit will be different for each individual assessor, depending on evidence used during internal quality assurance. However, your attendance at standardisation meetings is paramount to the quality of the training offered to your candidates.

The A2 award

As we have discussed, the A2 award is designed for those wanting to undertake assessment only. The elements within this award are:

A2.1 Agree and review plans for assessing candidates' performance.
A2.2 Assess candidates' performance against the agreed standards.
A2.3 Assess candidates' knowledge against the agreed standards.
A2.4 Make an assessment decision and provide feedback.

You will be involved in many similar activities to those for the A1 award, such as:

- observation of staff members
- assessing performance
- assessing knowledge and how this knowledge is applied
- making and recording assessment decisions
- giving feedback to the candidate.

As you look through the NOS for this award you will see that many of the requirements are the same as for the A1 award and therefore much of the above stated information applies to this award as well as the A1 award. For example, *A2.1 Agree and review plans for assessing candidates' performance* requires three assessment plans and two written reviews, which is the same as *A1.1* with the omission of a record of written or spoken explanation, while *A2.2 Assess candidates' performance against the agreed standards* requires three assessment decisions and a record of a professional discussion, which is the same as *A1.2*.

Who's who?

When working towards the A1 and A2 award, there will be a number of personnel involved in the process.

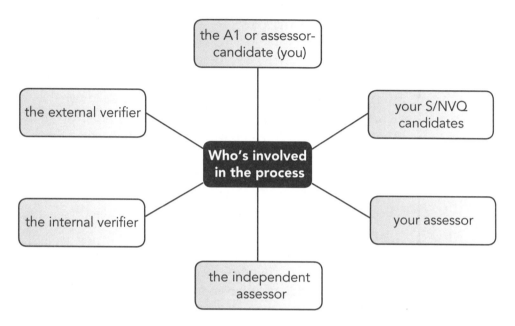

The A1 candidate (you)

This is your award and, as such, you should take ownership of your learning. You will be guided and supported by your assessor and possibly tutors, but the responsibility lies with you to gather and reference your evidence to prove your competency as an assessor. You must also prove that you have sufficient **occupational competence** to ensure an up-to-date working knowledge of the childcare sector, and be capable of carrying out the functions covered by the units you are assessing to the standard described within them according to current best practice. You must demonstrate how you have experience of the Principles and Values specified within the CCLD (see Chapter 1, pages 31–32).

The CCLD assessment strategy states that all assessors must:

- Have the necessary competence in the subject matter of the National Occupational Standards. They must also have the necessary competence in the assessment procedures and language(s) used for assessment. They must be occupationally experienced and competent i.e. be capable of carrying out the functions covered by the units they are assessing to the standard described within them according to current best practice. This competence should be credible and maintained through continuing professional development including professional updating where this is necessary to cover the extended children's age range.
- Hold, or be working towards the appropriate assessor qualification (hold D32 and 33 or hold or be working towards A1), to be achieved according to regulatory requirements. Where assessors do not yet hold a qualification their assessment decisions and activities must be reviewed and countersigned by a fully qualified assessor.
- Have knowledge of and commitment to the principles and values of the sector and the Principles and Values contained within the NOS.
- Have a thorough knowledge of the sector and its settings, including current legislative and regulatory requirements, codes of practice and guidance within the home country where assessment is taking place.

> ## Occupational competence
>
> Having held a post for a minimum of one year within the last two years that involved performing the activities defined in the standards as an experienced practitioner
>
> *OR*
>
> Being an experienced trainer or instructor of at least one year's standing in the competence area of the standards.

Therefore, you must have worked within the contexts of the CCLD standards for at least 12 months, during the last two years. This may have been as a nursery nurse, playworker, family worker or other role that is relevant to the CCLD NOS. As the CCLD NOS cover a huge range of job roles and responsibilities, particularly at Level 3, it may be necessary for more than one assessor to work with a CCLD candidate. This is to ensure that the assessor has the appropriate occupational competence to deliver the units required by the CCLD candidate. With this in mind, it is essential that a strong link is built between assessors and that standardisation meetings are successful in ensuring these links. The use of e-portfolios could also assist in ensuring continuity here, as assessors can work together with the same candidate from different venues. This competence should be credible and maintained through continuing professional development, including professional updating where this is necessary to cover the extended children's age range.

Over to you!

Occupational competence

Consider the occupational competence required by assessors of the following units, and the previous experience they may have had. How could the assessors maintain this competence, and update to cover the extended age range? The first one has been done for you as an example.

Table 4 How to maintain occupational competence

Unit	Assessor's possible previous job role/ experience	Ways to maintain competence
CCLD 309 – Plan and implement curriculum frameworks for early education	• Nursery nurse in early years unit within a school • Primary school teacher curriculum leader	• Attending training on curriculum frameworks • Work-shadowing curriculum manager at nursery school
CCLD 315 – Contribute to supporting parents with literacy, numeracy and language needs		
CCLD 316 – Maintain and develop a childminding business		
CCLD 321 – Support children with disabilities or special educational needs and their families		
CCLD 336 – Contribute to childcare practice in group living		
CCLD 345 – Help pupils to develop their literacy skills		
CCLD 327 – Support children who have experienced trauma		

Updating occupational competence can be done in a variety of ways. Assessors should update their competence continually, with real work practice yearly. This updating may be done by:

- carrying out a work placement
- job shadowing
- technical skill update training
- studying for learning and development units
- study related to job role
- collaborative working with awarding bodies
- attending courses.

It is important that you keep a record of competency update. This can be done simply using a template such as that shown in Table 5.

Over to you!
Updating occupational competence

Think about your current occupational competence, and where your areas of expertise lie. What could you do in order to update your competence to enable you to assess as many units as possible? Are your experience and background varied enough to cover the extended age range of 0–16 years? Plan how you might update your competence over the next two years.

Your candidates

You will need to be assessing a minimum of two CCLD candidates in order to gather evidence to prove your competence within the A1 award. Having more than two CCLD candidates will allow you to demonstrate your ability to work with a range of learners and adapt your assessments in accordance with their needs. For example, you might have a group of five CCLD candidates who are at different stages of their training, and therefore you might give more support and guidance to new candidates, while allowing more experienced candidates to take greater ownership of their learning.

You might have a candidate within your group who has additional learning needs, such as English as a second language. Using your work with this candidate as evidence towards your A1 will demonstrate how you can adapt assessment methods and evidence opportunities to suit the needs of the individual candidate.

Table 5 Continuous professional development record

Continuous professional development record				
Name		Position		
Date from		Date to		
Date	What I did	Why I did it	What I learnt from this	How I have used/ will use this

Your assessor

Your assessor will work with you to support you in planning assessments with your CCLD candidates, and assessing your competence during the assessment process. They will guide you through the process of S/NVQ assessment, making assessment decisions, providing feedback to your CCLD candidates and giving guidance on further actions. Your assessor will give you feedback on your work with your candidates and provide you with actions and guidance to help you develop your role further. You and your assessor will keep records and plans of the process, which should help you to navigate your way through the A1 award. Your assessor should also be involved in the quality assurance of the training centre, and may be carrying out internal verification of other awards. You may find that you have more than one assessor working with you throughout your A1 award. This is to meet the requirements for occupational competence for assessors and to ensure that the assessment process and delivery is flexible and personal to you. If this is the case, you will have a named assessor who will be known as the co-ordinating assessor. This co-ordinating assessor will be responsible for managing your assessment and the co-ordination of your award. They will be responsible for amalgamating, planning and directing assessment for your whole qualification, and will ensure that your award runs smoothly. The co-ordinating assessor will be responsible for making the final judgement of competence. You may find that your co-ordinating assessor works closely with the internal verifiers and will be involved with standardisation of the award and the assessment process.

Over to you!
A1 assessors

Think about how many A1 assessors will be involved in your award. Consider their occupational competence, and the individual roles they will play. Who will be your co-ordinating assessor and what specific skills or experience do they have?

The independent assessor

With any qualification, it is important to maintain quality standards and offer a balance of evidence to demonstrate competence. In order to do this, the A1 standards require part of the award to be independently assessed. The requirements for independent assessment state:

> 'This will require candidates (A1) to present a balance of evidence which must include a substantive component which has been assessed by someone who is independent from the candidate … Independent is defined here as a component job holder who is qualified as an assessor but will not act as the candidate's primary assessor.'

This means that someone other than your main assessor, who is independent from yourself, will assess part of your A1 award.

ENTO recommends that this evidence is best presented in the form of an assessment plan within Unit A1.1. Your assessor will discuss this with you further.

The internal verifier

Internal verifiers are the heart of the quality assurance processes within the S/NVQ system. There are three main aspects of the internal verifier's role:

1 verifying assessment
2 developing and supporting assessors
3 managing the quality of S/NVQ delivery.

The internal verifier will ensure consistent and reliable assessment and internal verification decisions, and will monitor the quality of assessment, highlighting any problems, trends or development needs of assessors. Your internal verifier will support your A1 assessor and check that their work is consistent. They will ensure that your assessor's decisions are accurate and reliable, and they will do this by regularly monitoring the quality of performance and arranging standardisation meetings.

Check it out

To find out more about internal verification processes, look at the *Joint Awarding Body Guidance on Internal Verification of S/NVQs*, which is available from QCA at www.qca.org.uk; www.sqa.org.uk

Check it out

To find out more about external verification, look at *External Verification of S/NVQs*, which is available from QCA at www.qca.org.uk; www.sqa.org.uk

The external verifier

The external verifier is employed by the awarding body to ensure that standards are being met coherently and consistently within all training centres that offer the A1 award. Their role is to monitor the work of approved training centres, and they provide the link between the awarding body and the centre. They will do this by:

- making sure that decisions on competence are consistent across centres
- making sure that the quality of assessment and verification meets the NOS
- providing feedback to centres
- making regular visits to centres and assessment locations
- ensuring that their own verification practice meets D35.

Quality assurance and standardisation

Quality assurance

A system under which an assessment team ensures that all services are of high quality and will satisfy the integrity of the award

Throughout the previous chapters, references have been made to 'quality assurance' or 'attending standardisation meetings'. This section will describe the role of quality assurance within S/NVQs and how this links with your assessor role. In order to understand how **quality assurance** affects your work, you must first understand what quality assurance is.

The term 'quality assurance' encompasses the processes that are adopted in order to maintain the required standards and to ensure consistency and improvement of working practices. Your centre is likely to have a *Quality Manual* that demonstrates all the ways in which quality is maintained and developed within your centre. Your centre may be involved in gaining recognition for its quality standards through projects such as Investors in People, ISO 9000, Matrix or Quality Mark Schemes.

Quality marks or schemes often have common features, including, for example:

Check it out

Find out more about quality schemes at www.ento.org.uk

- demonstrating a clear understanding of the organisation's objectives
- realising the potential of employees and their contributions
- effective communication systems
- demonstrating an understanding of employees' roles and expectations
- support mechanisms for reviewing and monitoring performance

- review and evaluation processes to facilitate continuous quality improvement
- commitment to equal opportunities.

The S/NVQ Code of Practice

The S/NVQ Code of Practice promotes quality, consistency, accuracy and fairness in the assessment and awarding of all S/NVQs. It works towards ensuring that standards are maintained in each occupational area and across awarding bodies from year to year.

The S/NVQ Code of Practice sets out:

- agreed principles and practice for the assessment and quality assurance of S/NVQs and S/NVQ units
- the responsibilities of S/NVQ awarding bodies and their approved centres in respect of the administration, assessment and verification of S/NVQs and S/NVQ units
- the basis upon which **ACCAC** and QCA will systematically monitor the performance of awarding bodies in maintaining the quality and standards across the S/NVQs they offer.

The internal verifier

With regard to the S/NVQ system, overall responsibility for quality assurance and standardisation lies with the internal verifier. The internal verifier is held accountable for the integrity and quality of the awards, and therefore must ensure that effective quality assurance procedures are in place and followed. Internal verification is a process of monitoring assessment practices to ensure that candidates receive fair and reliable assessments, which are consistently accurate and meet the requirements of the standards. Thorough internal verification ensures consistency, quality and fairness of assessment, marking, grading and feedback to candidates about their award.

Responsibilities of the internal verifier include:

- developing and maintaining policies and procedures to ensure effective assessment of the award
- training and supporting assessors and trainee assessors
- observation of assessor performance
- sampling portfolios
- evaluating the effectiveness and quality of assessment processes within the centre.

Check it out

Obtain your copy of the S/NVQ Code of Practice at www.qca.org.uk

ACCAC

The Qualifications, Curriculum and Assessment Authority for Wales

Your centre will hold their own internal verification policy or procedure, which will set out the guidelines for internal verification, which must be met by all staff.

Over to you!
Internal verification policies

Look at your centre's internal verification policy, and read through it, making sure that you understand it in its entirety. Consider the following.

- Does the policy set out clear guidance regarding the roles and responsibilities of staff involved in the S/NVQ process?
- Does it identify a sampling strategy?
- Does it include details of maintaining records?
- Does it demonstrate how candidates may appeal decisions, and how the appeals procedure should work?

It is important to remember that there is no set internal verification policy, and every centre will devise their own depending upon the staffing structures and resources within the centre.

Verifying assessment

Verifying assessment is undertaken to maintain the quality of assessment for candidates and can be broken down into three elements:

- **sampling** (reviewing the quality of assessors' judgements at both interim and summative stages)
- **monitoring practice** (ensuring that the national standards of assessment are met and adhered to)
- **standardising assessment judgements** (ensuring that assessors consistently make valid and fair decisions).

Summative sampling
Reviewing the quality of the assessment decision once the assessor has confirmed the unit/ portfolio is complete.

Interim sampling
Reviewing the quality of the assessment at various stages within the assessment process.

Standardisation

The term standardisation means to 'bring into conformity with a standard'. Within S/NVQs, standardisation is concerned with ensuring that assessors interpret the standards and assessor-candidates consistently and based on the same evidence. The standardisation process may take the form of monthly meetings, where assessors meet to discuss various units of the award, and standardise how competence will be achieved. The internal verifier plays the key role with regard to quality assurance in the delivery and assessment of S/NVQs, and may organise standardisation meetings.

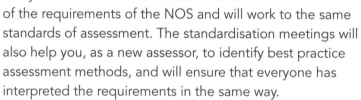

These meetings will provide an opportunity for assessors and internal verifiers to look at, and standardise, their practices within the centre, and to discuss how effective their assessment and delivery is. Some centres will focus on a particular unit of the S/NVQ at each meeting, looking at its requirements, and deciding how best to tackle the unit. These standardisation meetings ensure that everyone involved in the award is aware of the requirements of the NOS and will work to the same standards of assessment. The standardisation meetings will also help you, as a new assessor, to identify best practice assessment methods, and will ensure that everyone has interpreted the requirements in the same way.

Check your understanding

As you have reached the end of this chapter, you may find it useful to consolidate all that you have learnt by answering the following questions. You will find suggested answers in the back of the book on page 184.

1 If you have completed the A1 award, do you need to do the A2 award?
2 List five activities you might be involved in while working towards the A1 award.
3 How many elements are there within the A1 award?

4 How many candidates will you need to assess in order to gain your A1 award?

5 Why might you decide to only do the A2 award?

6 What subjects might your assessor cover during professional discussion?

7 Where could you obtain information about other Learning and Development awards?

8 What is the role of the external verifier?

9 Define the term 'summative sampling'.

10 What is the purpose of standardisation meetings?

Chapter 5

Developing reflective practice

Introduction

Throughout this book, you have been encouraged to think about your own practice and about the effects it has on your candidates and their experience. Working in a professional manner demands a continuous process of reflection, which involves looking at your practices, ideas and actions, then evaluating their effectiveness in order to make improvements.

The idea of reflective practice is relatively new, yet it can improve the quality of your work considerably. This chapter looks at how you can reflect on what you have learnt throughout this book, as well as during your time as a trainee assessor, and what this means for you as a qualified assessor.

The idea of reflection is to consider your actions and evaluate them, thinking about how they may have influenced those around you and how you might work differently to benefit your candidates and to develop your style and methods of working.

In Chapter 3, you looked at how to support your candidates and encourage them to reflect and evaluate their own learning. This chapter will help you to do the same with your own learning in order to fully develop your understanding of the role.

This chapter will help you to understand:
- how to reflect on practice
- how to develop reflective skills
- how to use reflection to challenge existing practice.

Reflecting on practice

Reflective practice

The process of thinking about and critically analysing your actions with the goal of changing and improving occupational practice.

Reflecting on your day-to-day practice enables you to analyse why and how you do things, and to consider whether other approaches might benefit you and your candidates. **Reflective practice** is used as a model for developing your skills and making sense of the work you do as an assessor. For example, you might reflect on a specific underpinning knowledge session and consider how you could have taught the information differently to enable better learning for the candidates.

Effective reflection requires you to be open-minded and to examine, question and assess your own practice, so as to develop your skills and knowledge. To develop your skills as a reflective professional, you should:

- listen openly to the ideas of others
- reflect on your own work and on the work of those around you
- consider and implement ways to develop your practice.

Experiences
Ideas
Understanding

Reflection
Re-evaluation

Outcome
Better practice
Application

The *experience* shown in the diagram above may be that of others as well as yourself, and it indicates the three stages of the reflection process:

1 think about your experience, understanding and ideas
2 reflect on what you have learnt from this experience
3 identify how this reflection will deliver outcomes and better practice, and how these will be applied.

Over to you!
Reflective practice

Consider how you have used reflective practice previously and how the reflection changed your outcomes. Think about how your practice improved and any impact this had on others around you.

Working in this reflective way allows you to take control of your learning and development as an assessor and to make changes in your practice that will develop your overall role.

Donald Schön (1996) made a remarkable contribution to our understanding of the theory and practice of learning. His theory on *reflection-in-action* has become part of the key ideology surrounding reflective learning, particularly the professional's ability to *think on their feet*. Schön wrote a series of books around the processes and development of reflective practitioners.

This ability to understand and change the situation is one which develops over time, as you become more confident in your own judgement. You will begin to reflect with the speed and spontaneity required by each situation, and make quick decisions as and when required. As a reflective practitioner, you would then make time to carefully consider the situation and response after the event, and question your actions by asking the following questions.

- What action did I take that worked, and why?
- What action did I take that did not work, and why?
- What could I have done differently, and how will I ensure that I do this next time a similar situation arises?

Schön describes this as reflecting on your knowledge-in-practice.

This preparation allows you to be prepared should the same event, or one similar, occur in the future. It entails evaluating your initial actions and determining what action you might take next time.

The best person to help you to work effectively within your role is yourself. Being a reflective practitioner means being aware of your limitations and the gaps in your knowledge, as well as your strengths and qualities.

Case study Dave Smith

Dave has been an assessor for a private training provider for two years. He thoroughly enjoys his work with the 16–18-year-old age group, but wants to take on more responsibility. His manager has asked him to attend a briefing day for internal verifiers with a view to his taking the V1 qualification. Dave is unsure of whether or not he wants to go. Although he feels ready for more responsibility, he is not sure if he is ready to be an internal verifier.

Dave agrees to go along to the briefing day and, while there, he enjoys learning about the quality assurance processes and standardisation. He feels more confident and aware of an internal verifier's role and responsibilities. He realises that his lack of understanding was probably affecting the way he worked with his candidates and internal verifier. Dave asks his line manager if he can attend a further course on quality assurance.

Think about . . .
1 Why is Dave becoming a reflective practitioner?
2 How might he benefit from becoming more aware of his practice?
3 How will Dave's candidates benefit from his deeper understanding?

Table 1 demonstrates how reflective practice can develop your work further.

Table 1 How reflective practice can develop your work further

Addressing candidates' needs	By thinking about the way you have responded to your candidates' individual needs, you can develop new strategies.
Working with colleagues	Reflecting on the way you interact with colleagues can help you to create better relationships. This can help you to enjoy your work more.
Your role with your candidates	By thinking about the effectiveness of the way you work with candidates, you can tailor your approach to suit their needs and interests.
Planning candidates' learning	By considering the effectiveness of your plans, you can help to develop new systems of planning and recording that are faster and more effective.
Working with external agencies	By thinking through how you work with external agencies, you may be able to develop stronger partnerships.

Benchmarks

Good practice requires time to evolve and develop and it is therefore important to evaluate your performance against **best practice benchmarks**. This is why it is essential that you continuously update your professional competence and undertake training to ensure that you are aware of changes in legislation and standards.

Developing reflective skills

In order to fully develop your skills as a reflective practitioner, you need to question what you do and why you do it, rather than just doing what you have been told to do. You may find it helpful to consider the different elements of your job role and to look at them individually.

There may be times when you feel you are making good progress and working efficiently. At these times, you should ensure you think about what it is that is working well. What skills or knowledge have assisted your work? Are there any particular practices within your setting which have helped you to work successfully? Considering these things will allow you to reflect on the progress you are making and what it is that is helping you to progress. You may also have days where you feel nothing is going right. Again, you should consider why this is. Is it a lack of knowledge, lack of resources or poor understanding that has made things difficult for you? Are there certain practices within the setting that are difficult to conform with and, if so, could you come up with alternative methods of working?

> **Best practice benchmarks**
>
> Standards that are widely agreed as providing the most advanced, up-to-date thinking and practice against which you can measure what you are doing (not minimum standards). They may be statutory/regulatory or based on other requirements or research.

The diagram below demonstrates how you might approach reflective analysis.

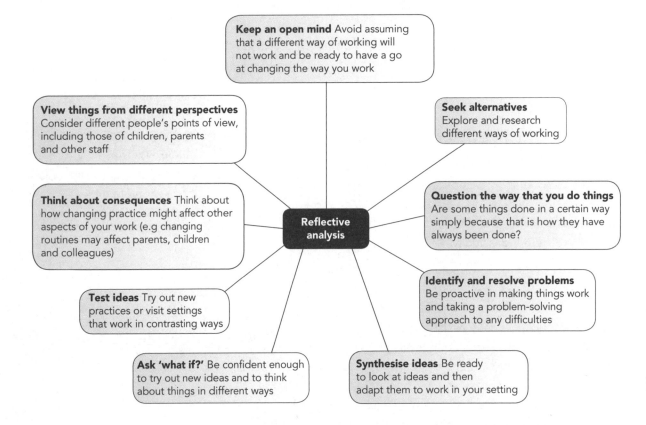

By using reflective processes as a tool for development, you will not only move forward in your own thinking, but may also support your colleagues to do the same.

You may occasionally find areas where there is only one appropriate response or approach; however, these are rare, as working with people demands flexibility and understanding of others' needs. The ability to reflect means considering other opportunities, approaches and possibilities, even if they are strange and unfamiliar. You may have come across professionals or colleagues who do not appear to like change and who say, 'But this is the way we've always done it.' It is important to recognise where things are going well; however, it is also important to understand that new curricula have been developed as well as new legislation and theories.

Case study College inspection

A local FE college recently went through its annual inspection. Overall the results were good, but the sector leader of the childcare department, Sally, was disappointed to find that their work with candidates with individual needs was only graded as satisfactory. Sally felt that this was a real strength. The staff in the childcare department had worked very hard and prided themselves on their hard work and dedication. Sally's first reaction was to blame the inspectors but, after a couple of days, she began to consider the practice within the team. She realised that there had been very little staff training or development on working with candidates with additional needs, and the Additional Needs Policy had not been updated for some years. The reason why this area had been overlooked was mainly that she had assumed that it was a strong area.

Think about . . .

1 Why is it important to regularly review your work?
2 How might the sector and the wider college benefit from reviewing this area of work?
3 How might individual staff benefit from focusing on this area of work?
4 What might be the benefits to the candidates?

Over to you!
The reflection process

Look into how your centre has changed over the last five years and consider the reflection processes that might have been carried out in order to make these changes.

Using reflection to challenge existing practice

Working within the training and development sector allows you to work alongside colleagues and professionals, rather than in isolation. For this reason, you may need to consult with others before changing and developing your own practice. This may involve using tact and diplomacy, as other staff may feel happy with their current practice.

You could begin by talking through your ideas with your internal verifier or line manager, asking for their opinions and support with implementing any changes. You could agree to review and evaluate any changes that you make so that their effects can be discussed with the rest of the assessment and verification team. Staff meetings or standardisation meetings may be a good place to present your ideas and proposals.

Keys to good practice
Challenging existing practice

- Talk through changes with the rest of the team.
- Listen to others' concerns and ideas.
- Explain reasons for and benefits of changing practice.
- Avoid making personal comments.
- Review and evaluate changes to practice.

Adapted from *S/NVQ Level 3 Handbook in Children's Care, Learning and Development*, published by Heinemann

Over to you!
Are you a reflective practitioner?

As you have seen, it is important to reflect on your own practice. Take a look at the statements below to assess whether or not you are a reflective practitioner. You might like to use this task with your candidates, as the statements all refer to the Performance Criteria for CCLD Level 3, Unit 304.1.

Table 2   Are you a reflective practitioner?

Statement	Always	Sometimes	Never
I monitor my processes, practices and the outcomes from my work.			
I evaluate my own performance using best practice benchmarks.			
I reflect on my interactions with others.			
I share my reflections with others and use their feedback.			
I use reflection to solve problems.			
I use reflection to improve my practice.			

Listening to others can provide you with vital information to assist you in reflecting upon your own practice. You should aim to listen carefully to feedback, and not become defensive or take the feedback personally. The key focus is to improve practice.

Being a reflective professional requires you to take the time to consider your work, reflect on its objectives and evaluate its outcomes. You should be learning from your experiences and applying this newfound knowledge to future situations. This is exactly the same message as the one you will be trying to send to your candidates while you support them through their award and encourage them to become reflective practitioners too.

Check your understanding

As you have reached the end of this chapter, you may find it useful to consolidate all that you have learnt by answering the following questions. You will find suggested answers in the back of the book on page 185.

1 What is meant by the term 'reflective practitioner'?
2 Why is it important to continuously update your skills and knowledge?
3 Give two ways in which you might gain feedback about your practice.
4 How might colleagues benefit from reflective practice?
5 How might your candidates benefit from reflective practice?
6 List three things you might do to develop your skills as a reflective practitioner.
7 What are the three stages of the reflection process?

Chapter **6**

Gathering evidence for the S/NVQ for Children's Care, Learning and Development

Introduction

As you have already discovered, many changes have been made to the National Occupational Standards (NOS) during the revision of the Early Years Care and Education (EYCE) NOS and subsequent introduction of the Children's Care, Learning and Development (CCLD) NOS. Some of these changes have a substantial impact on the way you might assess the award, while others are more subtle. In order to fully encompass all assessment opportunities, you will need to understand the requirements of each unit, and to consider the most effective ways of supporting your candidates in demonstrating their competence towards the standards. You have already considered the importance of using a holistic approach and how to gather evidence in a variety of ways. This chapter will look at the differences in the new standards, and how they will impact on the assessment opportunities available. You will think about how you can encourage your candidates to gather evidence towards particular units of the award, and consider the appropriateness of such methods based on the placement your candidate is in.

This chapter will help you to understand:
- the requirements of particular units
- the opportunities for assessment towards these units.

The requirements of particular units

Within Chapter 1, you looked at some of the changes within the standards as they moved from Early Years Care and Education (EYCE) to Children's Care, Learning and Development (CCLD). Section 1 demonstrates this in more detail for the Level 2 award, in order to help you understand how the changes have impacted on the delivery of the new standards.

Section 2 looks at the units within the Level 3 award.

As you will see, the range of units within Level 3 provides scope for all practitioners at all levels to find units that are appropriate to them and their individual job roles. Observation of candidates towards these units will be as individual as they are, and no two observations will ever be the same!

Over to you!
Direct observation

Take a look at this direct observation. Consider which units of the Level 2 CCLD the candidate has demonstrated competence for and reference it to the Performance Criteria. Some have already been done for you as an example.

The Arches Training Centre

Assessment Plan

Candidate Name: David Jones   **PIN No:** 06/123456   **Programme:** CCLD Level 2

Assessment Date: 16th July 2006   **Time:** 11:00   **Place:** The Arches Play Centre

Pre-assessment Arrangements David in summer playscheme with children aged 8–14 years. One child with hearing impairment, using BSL as primary communication.

Record of observation	Reference
On arrival, David was sitting with a group of 4 children, assisting them with a creative activity. The children were painting and decorating 'jewellery boxes'. The children were sitting comfortably and within reach of the activity table. David supported the children involved, telling them how nice the boxes were, commenting on particular things the children were doing and praising their efforts. A child came to the table, and began to sign to David. David signed back, using facial expressions, and the child joined the activity. David explained to me that the child had asked if he could join in and David had encouraged him to do so, explaining what it was they were doing. The other children in the group were obviously comfortable with the child, and used basic signs to communicate with him.	206.3 1, 2, 3, 4
David's supervisor asked him to prepare the snack table for snacks. David checked what was for snacks that day, and checked the allergies form to ensure that all the children present could enjoy the snack provided. David laid out fresh fruit – apples, pears and oranges – jugs of juice and digestive biscuits. All the children were then instructed to wash their hands and line up for snacks. The children all did this independently. After having snacks, David took a group of mixed gender children into the sports hall to play volleyball; this was requested by the children. David explained all the rules to the group, and ensured that laces were tied and top buttons loosened to ensure health and safety. David suggested he be the referee and observed the game throughout, demonstrating how to play fairly and encouraging good sportsmanship. At one point, a younger child looked out of breath and red faced. David asked him quietly if he was OK, and suggested he sat out for a while. The boy explained that he had asthma and carried his inhaler in his bag. David asked an older child to go with the boy to get his inhaler, so that he didn't have to leave the rest of the group unsupervised.	

(Continued)

Over to you! *(Continued)*

Direct observation

Consider how David's assessor might confirm his knowledge during this observation. Which other types of evidence might the assessor use alongside this observation?

Changes from EYCE to CCLD for Level 2

CCLD Level 2 unit: 201 Contribute to positive relationships

Elements:
1 Interact with and respond to children
2 Interact with and respond to adults
3 Communicate with children
4 Communicate with adults

This unit should allow your candidate to consider appropriate ways of interacting with both the children and adults they come into contact with. They will think about verbal and non-verbal communication, along with equality and confidentiality. This unit can easily be directly observed via a number of holistic opportunities. For example, the candidate might be working with a child who has been bullied, helping them to develop confidence and self-esteem. By helping the child to work through their feelings, being empathetic and perhaps demonstrating ways of dealing with their feelings, the candidate will be demonstrating competence for 201.1 and 201.3. If the candidate then feeds this information back to the class teacher or parent, listening to further advice or instruction, showing respect and maturity, then they may show competence for the rest of the unit. An observation of this kind might then link into other units when written holistically, such as 202, 203, 207, 210.

CCLD Level 2 unit: 202 Help to keep children safe

Elements:
1 Prepare and maintain a safe and healthy environment
2 Follow procedures for accidents, emergencies and illness
3 Support the safeguarding of children from abuse
4 Encourage children's positive behaviour

EYCE related units: C2, C1, C7, E2

This unit encourages the candidate to demonstrate their competence in the safety and welfare of the children in their care. Due to the nature of this unit, direct observation cannot be planned in advance, so this unit will be observed holistically. The candidate needs to demonstrate that they understand how to respond in accordance with their setting's procedures during an accident or emergency. This might be observed during a water play session, for example. You might see the candidate preparing a water tray for a group of children. The candidate should check that the equipment is safe, and prepare the environment accordingly (202.1). The candidate would then carry out the activity with the group, praising positive behaviour and encouraging learning (202.4). If, during this activity, a child slips and has a bump, the candidate might respond and deal with the incident according to the procedures of the setting (202.2). The candidate might participate in child protection training, and the certificate could then be used as evidence towards 202.3. You might not have the opportunity to directly observe the candidate dealing with an emergency or illness, and therefore a witness statement from a senior staff member or a professional discussion will provide the key evidence for this unit. You might also feel it appropriate for the candidate to walk you through an evacuation of the setting, explaining exits and use of fire-fighting equipment, and demonstrating their knowledge of dealing with emergencies.

CCLD Level 2 unit: 203 Support children's development

Elements:
1 Contribute to supporting children's physical development and skills
2 Contribute to supporting children's emotional and social development
3 Contribute to supporting children's communication and intellectual development
4 Contribute to planning for children's development needs

EYCE related units: C1, E1, E2

This unit should be directly observed relatively easily, as the placements your candidates are in will be providing opportunities for the development of children's skills. The candidate will need to be taught how to correctly observe children using a variety of methods. This might be done through in-house training or on a one-to-one basis. Once they can do this, they should carry out their observations within their settings, and implement activities according to the findings of their observations. You will need to prepare and carry out a professional discussion with your candidate in order to ensure that they understand the need for child observations, and have a basic outline of the expected pattern of children's development across the 0–16 age range.

CCLD Level 2 unit: 204 Use support to develop own practice in children's care, learning and development

Elements:
1 Make use of support systems to develop your practice
2 Use new knowledge and skills to improve your practice

EYCE related unit: CU10

Within this unit, the candidate should demonstrate their ability to improve and develop their skills and performance within their role. As this unit looks at the candidate using support, you might feel it beneficial to use an expert witness at this stage. For example, your candidate's line manager might be the expert witness, and might have carried out an appraisal with the candidate. This could be used to evidence this unit, with questioning or a professional discussion covering any gaps, or substantiating alternative evidence. The candidate could write a reflective account about the training they have been involved in and how this has enhanced their practical work.

CCLD Level 2 unit: 205 Prepare and maintain environments to meet children's needs

Elements:
1 Prepare and maintain the physical environment
2 Prepare and maintain a stimulating environment
3 Maintain an environment that builds children's confidence and resilience
4 Support routines for children

EYCE related units: C1, E1, E2

Here, the candidate needs to demonstrate awareness of the importance of a child's environment. An example of this would be a candidate who is placed with a childminder, where space is limited within the childminder's home. This would be observed holistically, as all observations within the environment should show how the candidate has thought about the physical space for the activity and ensured health and safety at all times. It might be that wall displays are not appropriate within this environment, and therefore the candidate can be creative in making book or table displays, or making scrap books of children's work for them to look at. Again, through holistic observation, the candidate should be demonstrating their ability to encourage and support the children and work with the childminder, implementing consistent routines for the children and supporting their personal care.

CCLD Level 2 unit: 206 Support children's play and learning

Elements.

1 Participate in activities to encourage communication and language
2 Provide opportunities for children's drama and imaginative play
3 Encourage children to be creative
4 Support physical play and exercise
5 Encourage children to explore and investigate

EYCE related units: C8, C9

This unit may be one which is easily planned in advance, and allows for many other units to be observed holistically at the same time. For example, a candidate might be working with a group of children in a holiday playscheme. They might be making masks to use for the end of holiday performance (206.2, 206.3). While supporting the children with this task, the candidate could be chatting to the children about what they are making and encouraging communication skills within the group (206.1). The candidate might also support a group with a game of football, demonstrating behaviour strategies and ensuring equality of opportunity (206.4). The candidate might organise a 'bug hunt' and then ask the children to identify what they have found by looking it up on the internet (206.5).

CCLD Level 2 unit: 207 Contribute to the effectiveness of teams

Elements:
1 Agree and carry out your role and responsibilities within the team
2 Participate effectively as a team member

EYCE related unit: CU10

This unit should require very little planning for observation, as the candidate should be demonstrating competency for this unit throughout all observations. Demonstrations of team working and carrying out their role effectively should be done holistically, not be set up. A professional discussion with your candidate can then confirm that they understand the requirements on equality, diversity, discrimination and rights when working in teams and can demonstrate an understanding of appropriate legislation.

CCLD Level 2 unit: 208 Support the development of babies and children under 3 years

Elements:
1 Observe babies or children under 3 years as part of your everyday work
2 Provide safe physical care for babies and children under 3 years
3 Provide play activities that encourage learning and development
4 Communicate with, respond to and interpret the needs of babies or children under 3 years

EYCE related units: C12, C13

This is an ideal unit for candidates working in a baby room at a nursery, with a childminder, or alongside a health visitor, for example. Again, this can be planned in advance and the candidate should demonstrate their understanding of children within this age range. A professional discussion with the candidate after directly observing them with the babies will clarify any questions, and confirm their understanding of working with babies. You might find it beneficial to link this unit with other mandatory units during

your holistic observations. For example, 208.1 will link with 203 as it is about observing children, 208.2 links well with 202, and 208.3 links with 206. It is essential that you ensure the candidate fully demonstrates competence across all knowledge statements. For example, the candidate may demonstrate sterilisation of bottles with a microwave steriliser; however, they should be able to inform you of other methods of sterilisation that they might come across in other settings. A professional discussion with the candidate after an observation will allow you to determine their level of understanding. For example, why did they choose that particular activity, how does it link to the setting's planning, and what were the learning aims for the activity?

CCLD Level 2 unit: 209 Support a child with disabilities or special educational needs

Elements:
1 Support a child with disabilities or special educational needs by providing care and encouragement
2 Provide support to enable the child to participate in activities and experiences
3 Support the child and family according to the procedures of the setting

Throughout this unit, the candidate needs to demonstrate their ability to support a child with a disability or special educational needs. Your candidate does not have to be placed within a special school for this unit; however, they must work in a setting whose main purpose is to support the care, learning and development of children, working alongside their families or, if they work with a disabled child or a child with special educational needs, normally as an assistant in a setting. Again, you could link this unit with others, such as 206 and 208, depending on the setting and the children involved. During the assessment of this unit, the candidate needs to demonstrate their ability to support a child while adhering to the child's care plan and the policies and procedures of the setting. Due to the nature of this unit, it may be difficult to directly observe some elements, as you may find restrictions in place regarding confidentiality and the privacy and dignity of the child. In such a case, an expert witness will be invaluable in providing evidence of your candidate's skills and knowledge.

A professional discussion with your candidate based around legislation, integration, inclusion and equality should ensure that you have sufficient evidence to conclude the unit.

CCLD Level 2 unit: 210 Support children and young people's play

Elements:
1 Create a range of environments for children and young people's play
2 Offer a range of play opportunities to children and young people
3 Support children and young people's rights and choices in play
4 End play sessions

This unit is appropriate for candidates who work within young people's play environments, such as lunch-time supervisors, after-school clubs and holiday playschemes. The candidate needs to demonstrate that they are able to provide a range of activities and opportunities for risk, challenge and personal growth. A holistic direct observation within a suitable setting should provide the necessary evidence for this unit. The candidate might draw up questionnaires to ask the children their opinions on which activities to use, and then use these as a basis for activity planning. Reflective accounts from the candidate will demonstrate their ability to plan, carry out and reflect on their practice, and enable you to check their level of understanding.

Changes from EYCE to CCLD for Level 3

CCLD Level 3 unit: 301 Develop and promote positive relationships

Elements:
1 Develop relationships with children
2 Communicate with children
3 Support children in developing relationships
4 Communicate with adults

EYCE related units: E3, C2

Communicating and building relationships with children is something that should be observed throughout the award. During all assessments you should be looking for improvements in communication skills from the candidate and commenting on progression or the candidate's ability to differentiate between children. A professional discussion based on development in communication skills, communication adaptations, differentiation and the importance of building relationships should enable the candidate to demonstrate their knowledge and skills for this unit.

CCLD Level 3 unit: 302 Develop and maintain a healthy, safe and secure environment for children

Elements:
1   Establish a healthy, safe and secure environment for children
2   Maintain a healthy, safe and secure environment for children
3   Supervise procedures for accidents, injuries, illnesses and other emergencies

This unit requires the candidate to demonstrate how their environment promotes children's health, safety and protection. The candidate might walk you through evacuation procedures, demonstrating how they would support the children during an emergency. Reflective accounts will provide good evidence towards the requirements for outings and trips and for the safety of visitors. A statement from the expert witness could provide evidence of the candidate dealing with an ill child or an accident. This could also be in the form of a witness testimony from the teacher on duty at the time of the incident. Candidates should also attend first aid training and submit a copy of their certificate to demonstrate knowledge in the knowledge and understanding specifications (KUS).

CCLD Level 3 unit: 303 Promote children's development

Elements:
1   Observe development
2   Assess development and reflect upon implications for practice
3   Plan provision to promote development
4   Implement and evaluate plans to promote development

For this unit, your candidate needs to demonstrate competence in observing and assessing children's and young people's development and a plan to promote this development. It is important to note that the candidate will need to demonstrate competence in the full 0–16 age range, which might be done through professional discussion, reflective accounts or assignment work. The candidate will firstly need to understand the types of observation they could carry out and how to decide which is appropriate for which situation. It is anticipated that, at this level, the candidate will be involved in children's assessments and planning meetings with other staff within the setting. The expert witness might prepare a statement that identifies the candidate's strengths and inputs into such planning meetings. It might not be appropriate for you to observe the candidate carrying out observations on a child, and therefore submissions of these observations (with identifying factors removed) may be appropriate alongside a professional discussion to verify knowledge across the age range.

CCLD Level 3 unit: 304 Reflect on and develop practice

Elements:
1 Reflect on practice
2 Take part in continuing professional development

Reflective practice and self-assessment should be encouraged throughout the award, to enable the candidate to make judgements on their work and so make further improvements. Candidates should demonstrate their understanding of national procedures and the benchmarks for good practice which they are working towards. Professional discussion is an effective method for evidence here and you can encourage the candidate to reflect upon situations which you have observed and encourage them to evaluate their methods. By understanding their best practice benchmarks, candidates can demonstrate how they are working towards best practice, as well as how they might use feedback from others to evaluate their work. Candidates could provide reflective accounts to demonstrate this in practice. Where a candidate has received appraisals or continuous professional development discussions, copies of any paperwork can be submitted to their portfolio as evidence of ongoing development.

CCLD Level 3 unit: 305 Protect and promote children's rights

Elements:

1 Support equality of access
2 Implement strategies, policies, procedures and practice for inclusion
3 Maintain and follow policies and procedures for protecting and safeguarding children

EYCE related units: C17, C15

This unit allows the candidate scope to demonstrate their understanding of the importance of promoting children's welfare. An example of this could be with a candidate working within a Sure Start Children's Centre. You might be able to observe the candidate welcoming prospective parents into the centre, showing them around and ensuring that they are aware of the workings of the centre and the range of services available for them. The candidate might discuss access, equality and provision with the family. From this, you could question the candidate about the provision, encouraging them to reflect on the service and consider how the service might become more inclusive to members of the local and wider community. The candidate also needs to demonstrate understanding of child protection procedures and might do this through attending child protection training and then verbally demonstrating how they might put this knowledge into practice. Some settings may not easily lend themselves to direct observation of this kind, in which case candidates could prove competence through expert witness testimonies or professional discussion.

CCLD Level 3 unit: 306 Plan and organise environments for children and families

Elements:

1 Plan and provide an enabling physical environment for children
2 Organise space and resources to meet children's needs
3 Provide a caring, nurturing and responsive environment
4 Facilitate children's personal care

EYCE related units: E3, C2

The candidate needs to demonstrate their ability to organise the physical environment in accordance with the setting's policies and procedures and with statutory regulations. A professional discussion should allow the candidate to demonstrate their awareness of such policies and regulations, and holistic observation will allow you to see this within the context of their practice. There should be no need to plan a specific observation for this unit, as it should be observed through all situations. For example, you might arrange to observe your candidate carrying out a physical playtime with a group of children. The candidate should be aware of their surroundings and of provision for the safety of the children with regard to the physical space. After the observation, you might encourage the candidate to reflect on their practice and consider alternative ways of providing a safe physical environment. The last two elements of the unit, looking at care of the child, should again be observed holistically. Where observation is not appropriate, within the constraints of personal care, for example, reflective accounts or professional discussions would be appropriate.

CCLD Level 3 unit: 307 Promote the health and physical development of children

Elements:
1 Plan and implement physical activities and routines for children to meet their physical development needs
2 Plan and provide food and drink to meet the nutritional needs of children
3 Promote children's healthy physical development

EYCE related units: C2, C3

Promotion of health and physical development of children should again be holistic in its approach. The candidate will need to demonstrate knowledge across the age range. This unit links well with 306 and you might find it useful to observe the two units holistically. Your candidate should have no problem demonstrating their competence within real-work situations for this unit, as they will be providing physical opportunities in most settings. Candidates should demonstrate that they fully understand the importance of physical development, and a question and answer session might be appropriate at the end of the observation. The candidate needs to show an understanding of cultural diversity regarding food provision and activities, and this may be done through a project or assignment.

CCLD Level 3 unit: 308 Promote children's well-being and resilience

Elements:
1 Enable children to relate to others
2 Provide a supportive and challenging environment
3 Enable children to take risks safely
4 Encourage children's self-reliance, self-esteem and resilience

EYCE related unit: C5

Again, this unit can and should be carried out holistically during observations that have been planned around other units. Candidates at this level should be considering children's well-being and resilience throughout their day-to-day work, and therefore this should be holistically observed. Encouraging children to be empathetic, co-operative and safe is routine in all settings, and therefore candidates will be doing this automatically. For example, you might be observing a playworker working with a group of children with disabilities. The candidate might be setting up a treasure hunt for the group and might ask the group to decide on the rules and boundaries of the game, listening to their opinions and encouraging them to work together, considering the others in the group (308.1). The candidate might then carry out the treasure hunt with the group, supporting them through the game and encouraging them to try new experiences (308.2). The candidate might encourage the children to take safe risks and experience challenges while being supported and encouraged, treating the group with respect, dignity and consideration (308.3, 308.4). A professional discussion with the candidate should be based around risk assessment and supporting children based on their individual needs and abilities.

CCLD Level 3 unit: 309 Plan and implement curriculum frameworks for early education

Elements:
1 Prepare curriculum plans according to requirements
2 Implement curriculum plans

3 Monitor and reflect on implementation of curriculum frameworks

EYCE related unit: M7

Within this unit, your candidate needs to demonstrate a thorough understanding of early education frameworks and how to develop curriculum plans around the needs of the young children they are caring for. Therefore, this unit is more suited to candidates within an educational setting with younger children. Your candidate should be working within the appropriate framework for their home country. The candidate needs to demonstrate the implementation of their plans and the evaluation of the plans and, as such, this unit links nicely with Unit 304. This unit also links well with 303, as the observations made by the candidate will feed into and impact upon the curriculum plans they develop. Evidence for this unit can be gained through observation of the candidate during a planning meeting, demonstrating their ability to offer suggestions, draw on their knowledge of child development and individual children, and work with the rest of the team to develop the curriculum plan. Further evidence might be in the form of samples of the plan and a professional discussion of how the plans have been drawn up, implemented and reviewed. Witness testimonies could also be a source of evidence where direct observation has been unavailable.

CCLD Level 3 unit: 310 Assess children's progress according to curriculum frameworks for early education

Elements:
1 Identify and plan assessment requirements of curriculum frameworks
2 Assess and record children's progress in consultation with others

EYCE related unit: M7

This unit links directly with 309 above. It looks at the assessment of children's progress within the curriculum framework of the setting. The candidate needs to demonstrate their knowledge and understanding of formative and summative assessments and how to assess and record the progress of the children they are working with. Again, this unit links well with Unit 303, as the candidate makes assessments of the child in order to accurately plan for their learning. A professional discussion could be put to good use here. You could ask the candidate to bring copies of their child assessments with them to the meeting, as a basis for your discussion. The plans will allow the candidate to demonstrate why and how they carried out the assessment, and to evaluate the effects this might have had on the children they have been working with. The candidate can then discuss with you how they recorded the information gathered and how they worked in consultation with other team members. An expert witness account would also provide excellent evidence here, to demonstrate the candidate's knowledge and skills.

CCLD Level 3 unit: 311 Provide leadership for your team

Elements:
1 Outcomes of effective performance
2 Behaviours which underpin effective performance

EYCE related units: MCI, C4

Candidates taking this optional unit will need to be in a supervisory role, demonstrating their ability to manage, develop and motivate others. With the permission of all involved, direct observation towards this unit can be planned in advance. The ideal observation might be the candidate carrying out an appraisal or development meeting with another member of staff. The candidate could then reflect on the meeting and provide evidence in the form of a reflective account or you could hold a professional discussion after the meeting. The member of staff with whom the candidate has held the meeting could provide evidence in the form of a written statement, demonstrating how the candidate's leadership skills have supported and encouraged the staff member to move further within their role or career.

CCLD Level 3 unit: 312 Plan and implement positive environments for babies and children under 3 years

Elements:
1 Observe, assess and record developmental progress of babies and children under 3 years

2 Communicate with babies and children under 3 years to develop positive relationships
3 Plan and implement activities to enhance development
4 Exchange information and respond to parents' needs and preferences for their babies and children under 3 years

EYCE related unit: C14

Linking with 302, 303, 307 and 314, this unit is particularly aimed at candidates working with children under 3 years. This unit should ideally be observed holistically, watching the candidate interact with the children they are caring for and making provision for their learning and development. Once again, the candidate needs to demonstrate their ability to observe, assess and record the progress of the babies in their care and, as such, samples of these plans could be submitted as evidence. Observation of your candidate sharing information with parents should always be done with the prior consent of the parent involved. Where this is not available, a witness statement will provide adequate evidence for this element.

CCLD Level 3 unit: 313 Support early intervention for the benefit of children and families

Elements:
1 Help to identify families in need of early intervention and support
2 Negotiate and assess needs in consultation with families
3 Work with families and other agencies to access specialist support
4 Monitor and evaluate services to ensure the needs of children and families are met

This unit is particularly aimed at candidates who are responsible for supporting children and families in need of early intervention. Candidates should also assist professionals in implementing strategies and plans to meet the individual needs of families and children. The sensitive nature of this unit may make it difficult to directly observe, so you might find that using an expert witness makes evidencing this easier. The expert witness might observe the candidate working with families in need and be able to evidence how the candidate has worked alongside other professionals in order to support the children and families they are working with. Candidates could also provide reflective accounts of their work with families, all of which should remain confidential, having identifying factors removed. Professional discussion with the candidate will help you to ensure that the candidate has all the necessary knowledge and understanding required by the unit and with regard to confidentiality and work ethics.

CCLD Level 3 unit: 314 Provide physical care that promotes the health and development of babies and children under 3 years

Elements:
1 Provide a safe and secure environment for babies and children under 3 years
2 Provide for the nutritional needs of babies and children under 3 years
3 Supervise and use physical care routines to promote development
4 Provide an emotionally secure and consistent environment
5 Recognise and respond to illness in babies and children under 3 years

Linking well with 312, this unit requires the candidate to demonstrate their ability to provide care for children and babies in partnership with the parents. Candidates choosing this optional unit should be working in a supervisory role with children aged 3 and under.

Elements 1, 2, 3 and 4 should all be easily observed holistically, as the processes involved should all happen on a daily basis. Where candidates do not make the bottle feeds within the setting, for example, the candidate needs to show they understand and are able to perform the task, which may be through professional discussion, simulation or assignment. Element 5 is less likely to be observed, as many settings do not allow poorly children to attend. Here an expert witness could write an account of a time when the candidate cared for a child who had become poorly while within the setting, and detail the response and actions of the candidate. The candidate could submit a chart detailing common illnesses and actions they would take for these. A recognised first aid certificate would also provide evidence here.

CCLD Level 3 unit: 315 Contribute to supporting parents with literacy, numeracy or language needs

Elements:
1 Identify and encourage parents with some literacy, numeracy or language needs to improve their skills
2 Provide information for parents to enable them to access support
3 Reflect on and evaluate own and organisational practice in supporting parents

This optional unit is particularly useful for candidates who have a role in identifying parents with literacy, numeracy or English for Speakers of Other Languages (ESOL) needs and signposting them to local learning opportunities. Candidates might be working within any childcare setting, but particularly Children's Centres, youth clubs and community groups. Candidates need to demonstrate an understanding of, and a commitment to, supporting parents' needs, and recognising how to work with parents in a way that is non-judgemental and non-stereotypical. Again, the sensitivity of this unit might mean that observation is not necessarily the most effective form of evidence, so professional discussion about a particular scenario or an expert witness statement would be more beneficial. Candidates could submit work to demonstrate their understanding of the support mechanisms in place for families in their area and talk through some of the work that has been done with particular families. The final element of this unit links with 304, asking candidates to reflect on their practice. This is likely to be best done during a professional discussion, as you can encourage the candidate to reflect on a particular aspect of their work within this unit.

CCLD Level 3 unit: 316 Maintain and develop a childminding business

Elements:
1 Provide information about your childminding business
2 Administer your childminding business

This unit is specifically targeted at childminders, allowing scope for investigation into the local market and understanding of related advertising. This unit is very straightforward, and much of it can be evidenced through professional discussion and direct observation of the products created by the candidate. The candidate will need to demonstrate their knowledge of the tax system and how to efficiently run a business. As it is likely that the candidate will be working alone, scope for use of expert witnesses will be limited, and therefore you may find that observation of practice and work products will provide the evidence for this unit. However, the candidate may be part of a childminding network, in which case network co-ordinators could provide valuable evidence.

CCLD Level 3 unit: 317 Work with families to enhance their children's learning and development

Elements:
1 Liaise with families about their expectations of their child
2 Encourage families to be involved with their children's learning and development
3 Review children's progress with families

EYCE related unit: P2

This unit is particularly good for candidates who work with families to support their child's development. Examples of this would be speech therapy or behavioural support. Some of the information gathered during this unit may be sensitive and, as such, confidentiality should be stressed to the candidate. Candidates working with parents in this way need to demonstrate sensitivity and value the diversity of families, as well as have a thorough understanding of developmental milestones. Your candidate will need to show an understanding of family culture and how this may affect expectations put on the child. Professional discussion will allow the candidate to demonstrate these skills and knowledge, and allow you to draw this understanding from them, while maintaining the confidentiality of the families.

CCLD Level 3 unit: 318 Plan for and support self-directed play

Elements:
1 Collect and analyse information on play needs and preferences
2 Plan and prepare play spaces

3 Support self-directed play

4 Help children and young people to manage risk during play

As this unit focuses particularly on play, it is ideal for candidates working within play settings, such as holiday playschemes, before- and after-school clubs, and youth centres. An example of assessment towards this unit might be within the context of a candidate who is a youth club leader. The candidate might demonstrate to you how they have looked at the local needs for young people in the area and provided activities to meet this demand. This research could have been through a meeting with local young people or a survey (of which you can observe the product evidence) (318.1). During the activities with the children, you can observe how the candidate has prepared the play area and obtained resources in accordance with the research carried out (318.2). You can then observe the candidate playing alongside the children, supporting them in their play and managing risks (318.3, 318.4). Much of the evidence for this unit can be obtained through direct observation, as well as discussion with the candidate and the young people involved.

CCLD Level 3 unit: 319 Promote healthy living for children and families

Elements:

1 Enable children and families to identify healthy living options

2 Encourage and support children and families to implement healthy lifestyles

Candidates opting to do this unit should ideally be working with health professionals, supporting families to access information within the context of healthy living. An example of this might be a candidate who is working alongside a nutritionist within a family centre. The candidate can be observed working with families – providing permission has been obtained – to help them make healthy living choices. Candidates might be involved in cookery classes for families, health-awareness days or parent and toddler exercise sessions, all of which can be planned for direct observation. More evidence could be submitted through expert witness testimonies or reflective accounts.

CCLD Level 3 unit: 320 Care for children at home

Elements:
1 Implement the requirements of parents in line with current best practice guidance
2 Create positive environments for children within the home setting
3 Take children outside the home

This unit is ideal for childminders or nannies who look after children within the home environment, and childminders may link this with Unit 316. Element 1 is best observed during an initial meeting with a new parent – with prior permission – and allows the candidate to demonstrate their ability to negotiate terms which will support the care of the child and family. Element 2 can be observed holistically, as the content of the element should be demonstrated at all times while caring for children, and should come naturally to the candidate. Element 3 could be a planned trip with children or an outing to the library, for example, which should not take a great deal of planning, as outings should be an integral part of working with children. Criteria which are not observed can be easily covered through professional discussion or questioning with the candidate.

CCLD Level 3 unit: 321 Support children with disabilities or special educational needs and their families

Elements:
1 Contribute to the inclusion of children with disabilities or special educational needs
2 Help children with disabilities or special educational needs to participate in the full range of activities and experiences
3 Support families to respond to children's needs

EYCE related unit: C17

Candidates choosing this unit need to be working within a setting where they support the needs of a child and family with special needs. This does not necessarily mean working in a special school, as a childminder might have a child with special needs, as will mainstream settings. Candidates need to demonstrate a high level of understanding of a variety of needs of particular children, and may find it best to provide this in the form of written assignment work. However, the majority of this unit can be holistically observed where the candidate is working with children with special needs. A professional discussion will assist the knowledge process, as the candidate explains why they did a particular activity, with expert witness testimonies providing evidence where the nature is sensitive.

CCLD Level 3 unit: 322 Empower families through the development of parenting skills

Elements:
1 Promote parents' self-confidence in the parenting role
2 Encourage parents to relate positively to their children
3 Support parents in play activities with their children
4 Support parents in accessing information and community support

EYCE related unit: P4

Candidates choosing this unit are required to be within a setting that supports children in partnership with their families. Many settings will do this, especially in light of the *Every Child Matters* agenda which encourages parental partnership working. An example for this unit might be a candidate working with a fathers' group, supporting their parenting role. The candidate will develop positive, trusting relationships with the group in order for them to truly benefit from the experience, and provide opportunities for the group to share their concerns and experiences with each other (322.1). The candidate might then provide information, activities and support to the group to assist them in developing positive parenting skills (322.2, 322.4). It might be that the candidate provides opportunities for the fathers to put their learning into practice and offers play experiences with the children (322.3). A professional discussion after an observation of this kind would allow the candidate to demonstrate their understanding of the group, and the knowledge that led them to perform in the way they did.

CCLD Level 3 unit: 323 Use Information and Communication Technology to promote children's early learning

Elements:
1 Plan to use ICT in support of children's early learning
2 Implement ICT activities
3 Evaluate children's learning through ICT

This unit can be performed within any childcare setting in which ICT equipment is available. It is important that ICT is not just thought of as computers, but that the candidate demonstrates their ability to use a wide range of ICT equipment, such as cameras, DVD players, video recorders and telephones. Children can use ICT at all ages, and examples of opportunities to provide this may be through role play, sending digital cameras home for children to take photos of their family and share with others, or older children making a video of their community group activities. Whatever the activity, the candidate needs to show how they have planned the use of the equipment and where necessary how this fits into the overall curriculum planning for the setting. Candidates should then implement the activity with the children and evaluate its effectiveness. Evidence for this unit can be provided via direct observations for shorter activities, or by observation of product evidence – perhaps the editing of the video – for longer projects.

CCLD Level 3 unit: 324 Support the delivery of community based services to children and families

Elements:
1 Work with other professionals to deliver community services to families
2 Work with families to provide advice, guidance and support

Candidates choosing this unit need to be working alongside professionals within the community; for example, with a health visitor or community midwife. Due to the nature of the work, direct observation may not be an option and therefore professional discussion or expert witness testimonies will probably play a big part in this unit. You can observe the product evidence provided by the community visit, such as an action plan, as long as confidentiality is maintained.

CCLD Level 3 unit: 325 Support the child or young person's successful transfer and transition in learning and development contexts

Elements:

1 Plan for transfer and transition
2 Support the child or young person to prepare for transfer or transition
3 Monitor the success of transfer and transition and identify continued support needs

This is an ideal unit for candidates who are involved in supporting children through transitions, such as care workers supporting children within foster families. An example of evidence collection for this unit might be a candidate working alongside a care worker who supports young people during the transition from a care home into a foster family. The candidate might assess the needs of the child and the prospective family and match the two as closely as possible. They will work with the child and family to make the transition as smooth as possible. The candidate will demonstrate the required knowledge to make these judgements, and understand relevant legislation relating to this unit. Direct observation of this unit will be difficult due to the sensitive nature of the task, so professional discussion and expert witness testimonies will be the basis for the evidence within this unit.

CCLD Level 3 unit: 326 Safeguard children from harm

Elements:

1 Refer concerns about the welfare of children
2 Share information for the purpose of assessing children in need and their families
3 Support plans, interventions and reviews that safeguard children and promote their welfare

EYCE related unit: C15

The first product evidence for this unit will be a copy of a certificate from child protection training. It is advisable that training centres deliver such training to all candidates or refer candidates to external training providers to receive this knowledge. It is unlikely that this unit will have any direct observation, and therefore professional discussion should enable the candidate to demonstrate their understanding of child protection and the procedures they should follow should they need to. This unit links closely to Unit 305.

CCLD Level 3 unit: 327 Support children who have experienced trauma

Elements:
1 Recognise the needs of children who have experienced trauma
2 Respond to the needs of children who have experienced trauma
3 Seek support for your own practice and development

In order to carry out this unit, candidates need to be working closely with children and young people who have experienced trauma. An example of this might be as a playworker within a women's refuge. This is an extremely sensitive unit and observation would be unlikely. Professional discussion and expert witness testimonies would therefore provide the main source of evidence within this unit. Candidates will need to demonstrate their understanding of child development and how to work with children who have a variety of needs. The main importance of this unit is that the candidate is aware of legislation, policies and frameworks to which they should work in these instances.

CCLD Level 3 unit: 328 Administer provision within the childcare setting

Elements:
1 Maintain access procedures
2 Collect and store information
3 Administer budgets and financial arrangements, according to the procedures of the setting
4 Operate systems for the supply of materials and equipment
5 Supervise the work of others

EYCE related unit: M2

This unit looks at the day-to-day running of the childcare setting, and is suitable for most candidates. This unit is easily holistically observed. For example, you might have planned to observe the candidate carrying out a manipulative activity with play dough. On arrival, the candidate might greet you at the door and ask you to sign in, following all procedures for access to the setting (328.1). The candidate might then take the necessary equipment from the store cupboard, recording what they have taken and the amount of stock left (328.2). During the observation, a parent might approach and ask to settle the bill, which the candidate would do in accordance with the setting's procedures (328.3). The candidate could then show you product evidence of receipts, emails and order forms, demonstrating their ability to maintain stock and supply of materials (328.4). Candidates should also demonstrate their ability to supervise others, which will link directly to Unit 311.

CCLD Level 3 unit: 329 Work with a management committee

Elements:
1 Prepare and present operational plans and reports to management committees
2 Implement management committee policies and procedures
3 Work with management committees to identify funding streams

EYCE related unit: M20

Candidates wishing to carry out this unit need to be within a setting which is run by a management committee. Much of this unit is based on the preparation of plans, policies and procedures which can be submitted as evidence or observed as product evidence. A professional discussion with the candidate can draw out reasons behind specific decisions made in conjunction with the committee members. Applications for funding, emails, letters and faxes can all be observed as product evidence.

CCLD Level 3 unit: 330 Establish and maintain a service for children and families

Elements:
1 Identify and negotiate requirements with children and their families
2 Establish and maintain agreements with children and families

3 Establish and maintain systems for the exchange of information with children and families

4 Monitor and evaluate services to ensure the needs of children and families are met

EYCE related unit: P8

This unit focuses on providing specific services for children and their families and, as a result, most candidates could carry out this unit. With permission from families, this unit could have a planned direct observation when meeting with the parents to discuss their child's requirements before entering the setting. The candidate should demonstrate their ability to work with families, share information and develop agreements for the care of the child. The candidate needs to be in a supervisory role in order to carry out these tasks. Plans, agreements, letters and notes can all be observed as product evidence towards this unit. The candidate also needs to demonstrate knowledge of the current legislation, policies and procedures relating to this work, which may be evidenced during a professional discussion.

CCLD Level 3 unit: 331 Support children and families through home visiting

Elements:
1 Establish, develop and maintain relationships with families
2 Provide support to families
3 Liaise with colleagues, professionals and agencies to support families

EYCE related unit: P7

Candidates choosing this unit are required to be working in a capacity that allows them to visit families and children in their home. This might be as a counsellor, health visitor or support worker, for example. With permission from parents, much of this unit can be directly observed; however, where permission is not granted, it may be beneficial to use the expert witness as evidence. Any plans or products from the home visits may be observed as product evidence and confidentiality must be maintained throughout.

CCLD Level 3 unit: 332 Involve families in the childcare setting

Elements:
1 Provide information and establish relationships with families
2 Encourage families to attend and participate in groups
3 Monitor provision and evaluate the involvement of families

EYCE related unit: P5

Linking with Unit 322, this unit is ideal for any candidate who works to involve families within their setting. Candidates might provide information boards for parents with the information in a variety of formats and languages and may be observed welcoming parents into the setting and providing answers to queries (332.1). The second element may be observed during an open evening at the setting, or a parents' summer barbeque evening. This unit may easily be observed within the context of a playgroup, where parents are encouraged to attend on a rota to help the children within the group. Candidates should demonstrate their ability to make families feel welcome within the setting, and show a variety of methods that they could use to do so.

CCLD Level 3 unit: 333 Recruit, select and keep colleagues

Elements:
1 Outcomes of effective performance
2 Behaviours which underpin effective performance

Candidates wanting to do this unit need to have a lead or supervisory capacity within their setting. It may be possible, with permission from potential candidates, for you to observe your candidate carrying out an interview. Where this is not possible, witness testimonies from others involved in the interview process can provide evidence. Product evidence in the form of interview questions, advertisements, etc. can be used as evidence, while a professional discussion will allow the candidate to discuss retention and recruitment ideas within the setting, along with demonstrating an understanding of the dynamics within their team.

CCLD Level 3 unit: 334 Deliver services to children and families whose preferred language is not English or Welsh

Elements:
1 Work with children and families to assess communication needs
2 Establish and maintain communication to support service delivery
3 Monitor and evaluate communication support to ensure the needs of children and families are met

This unit looks at the delivery of services to families with English as a second language or those using alternative methods of communication, such as sign language. Candidates need to demonstrate their ability to provide an inclusive service, and may make adjustments to do so. This should be easily observed where such families are making use of the service. Expert witness evidence may also be of use here where observation is not possible. You could observe product evidence where a candidate has provided information in a different language, for example, or a copy of a sign language course certificate.

CCLD Level 3 unit: 335 Allocate and check work in your team

Elements:
1 Allocate and check work in your team

Linking closely with Unit 311, this unit allows candidates to demonstrate their ability to manage teams and support the dynamics of the team. Direct observation of this unit can be planned to be carried out during team meetings, as the candidate allocates workloads and shift patterns, and checks previous progress. A professional discussion with the candidate will allow them to explain why they made certain decisions and demonstrate their understanding of appropriate legislation and policy.

CCLD Level 3 unit: 336 Contribute to childcare practice in group living

Elements:
1 Contribute to planning, implementing and reviewing daily living programmes for children and young people

2 Work with groups to promote individual growth and development
3 Contribute to promoting group care as a positive experience

An ideal unit for candidates working in environments where children are living as a group, such as within boarding schools or care homes. Some of this work may be sensitive and therefore direct observation may not be appropriate. Candidates need to demonstrate their ability to work within the confines of this role, and may offer product evidence in the form of children's care plans, for example. This could be observed by you to confirm the candidate's ability within this context. You might be able to observe team planning meetings which the candidate is involved in to observe their knowledge of working with children who are in group living. Candidates may need to provide reflective accounts or assignment work in order that this unit be evidenced appropriately.

CCLD Level 3 unit: 337 Create environments that promote positive behaviour

Elements:
1 Implement behaviour policies, procedures and strategies
2 Promote positive aspects of behaviour

EYCE related unit: C7

All candidates working within a childcare setting should be able to carry out this unit. It should be holistically observed throughout the observations of other units as the candidate positively reinforces wanted behaviour and addresses negative behaviour in accordance with the policies and procedures of the setting. Where behaviour plans or progress charts have been developed, these can be observed as product evidence.

CCLD Level 3 unit: 338 Develop productive working relationships with colleagues

Elements:
1 Develop productive working relationships with colleagues

EYCE related units: MCI, C4

Linking with 311 and 335, this unit addresses how the candidate develops working relationships with colleagues. This should be observed holistically as the candidate works through their daily routine, supporting other team members and ensuring that roles are fully agreed. Candidates might talk with you about times when they have discussed their relationships with others in the team, or perhaps sorted out a disagreement.

CCLD Level 3 unit: 339 Co-ordinate special educational needs in early education settings

Elements:
1 Liaise with parents and other professionals in respect of children with special educational needs
2 Advise and support colleagues in the setting
3 Ensure that individual education plans for children are in place and regularly reviewed
4 Collect, record and update relevant background information about children with special educational needs

This unit is particularly aimed at the Special educational needs co-ordinator (SENCO) within the setting. For Element 1, observations carried out holistically can provide good evidence, particularly those linked to Unit 321. Evidence for Element 2 could be in the form of observations of team meetings. Where the candidate has carried out appraisals with a team member or given advice and guidance to a member of staff working with a particular child, the product evidence may be observed. Elements 3 and 4 can also be evidenced using observation of educational plans, and by providing the candidate with time to discuss how the plans are implemented and to review the effectiveness of such plans. Candidates can show you children's records and discuss how they are kept up to date and how they benefit the child and the family. All of the above must remain confidential and the permission of the parents needs to be obtained.

CCLD Level 3 unit: 340 Establish, develop and promote quality systems and procedures for the delivery of childcare services

Elements:
1 Establish quality systems for the delivery of childcare services

2 Maintain quality systems

3 Evaluate and review quality systems and procedures

This unit is appropriate for candidates who have responsibility for developing policies, procedures and systems within the setting. It is unlikely that evidence for this unit will be observed, and therefore product evidence, reflective accounts and expert witness testimonies will be the primary sources of evidence for this unit. This unit links very closely with Unit 341 below.

CCLD Level 3 unit: 341 Advise and mentor those implementing quality systems and procedures for the delivery of childcare services

Elements:

1 Identify quality assurance requirements

2 Support the collection of evidence

3 Support the development of practice to meet quality assurance requirements

See above.

CCLD Level 3 unit: 342 Meet regulatory requirements in the childcare setting

Elements:

1 Identify regulatory requirements

2 Plan for inspection, in consultation with colleagues

3 Collect required evidence

4 Take appropriate action to meet requirements

This unit looks at how the candidate ensures they meet the regulatory requirements for their setting. This might be in accordance with Ofsted guidance, for example. Candidates might demonstrate knowledge of this through professional discussion or might hold staff meetings to clarify queries, which you could directly observe. Where inspections are imminent, you could observe inspection meetings with staff and observe product evidence in terms of minutes from meetings or inspection reports. Candidates might draw up action plans in response to inspections, and this could be used as product evidence.

CCLD Level 3 unit: 343 Support learners by mentoring in the workplace

Elements:
1 Planning the mentoring process
2 Setting up and maintaining the mentoring relationship
3 Giving mentoring support

This unit is appropriate for candidates who are responsible for trainees within their setting. This unit should be observed holistically where available, as the candidate supports their trainee throughout the day-to-day running of the setting.

CCLD Level 3 unit: 344 Enable individual learning through coaching

Elements:
1 Coach individual learners
2 Assist individual learners to apply their learning

Candidates choosing this unit need to have a role that involves using coaching as a way of encouraging individual learning. This links very closely to Unit 343, above, as the candidate demonstrates their ability to give constructive feedback to their trainees, supporting the trainee's learning within the setting.

CCLD Level 3 unit: 345 Help pupils to develop their literacy skills

Elements:
1 Help pupils to develop their reading skills
2 Help pupils to develop their writing skills
3 Help pupils to develop their speaking and listening skills

EYCE related unit: C24

This unit is primarily for candidates working as classroom/teaching assistants. It is easily planned for observation, as literacy and numeracy are carried out within schools every day. You may wish to plan and observe 345 and 346 together. Product evidence provided by the candidate in the form of curriculum plans and support strategies could also be used as product evidence. A professional discussion with the candidate will ensure that they are aware of the curriculum and school policies within which they should be working.

CCLD Level 3 unit: 346 Help pupils to develop their numeracy skills

Elements:
1 Help pupils to develop their understanding and use of numbers
2 Help pupils to understand and use shape, space and measures

EYCE related unit: C25

See Unit 345.

Useful resources

Websites

www.dfes.gov.uk

> The Department for Education and Skills, established with the purpose of creating opportunity, releasing potential and achieving excellence for all.

www.qca.org.uk

> The Qualifications and Curriculum Authority (QCA) is committed to building a world-class education and training framework by regulating, developing and modernising the curriculum, assessments, examinations and qualifications.

www.surestart.gov.uk

> Sure Start is the government programme to deliver the best start in life for every child, bringing together early education, childcare, health and family support.

www.ento.org.uk

> ENTO (Employment National Training Organisation) offers development in the workplace through the use of National Occupational Standards (NOS) and other means, and recognises that development through formal accreditation results in the achievement of qualifications. It provides information, advice, guidance and support for those who use their NOS.

www.cwdcouncil.org.uk

> The Children's Workforce Development Council aims to improve the lives of children and young people. It does this by ensuring that the people working with children have the best possible training, qualifications, support and advice. It helps children's and young people's organisations and services to work together, so that the child is at the centre of all the services.

www.playwork.org.uk

> As the Playwork unit within SkillsActive, Playwork aims to raise the level of understanding about the importance of children's play, improve the access to good-quality play provision throughout England, set standards of excellence in education, training and qualifications and develop

opportunities for playworkers to access education, training and qualifications.

www.everychildmatters.gov.uk

Every Child Matters: Change for Children is a new approach to the well-being of children and young people from birth to age 19.

www.skill.org.uk

National Bureau for Students With Disabilities. Skill is a national charity promoting opportunities for young people and adults with any kind of disability in post-16 education, training and employment across the UK.

www.basic-skills.co.uk

Helping people of all ages who struggle with words and numbers in their everyday lives, by supporting those who teach them.

Government documents

- The Green Paper – Every Child Matters
- The Children's Workforce Strategy
- The Lead Professional Good Practice Guidance
- The Common Core of Skills and Knowledge
- The National Strategy for Improving Adult Literacy and Numeracy
- Joint Awarding Body Guidance for S/NVQs and VQs in Children's Care, Learning and Development

Other publications

- *S/NVQ Level 2 Children's Care, Learning and Development Candidate Handbook*, Heinemann
- *S/NVQ Level 3 Children's Care, Learning and Development Candidate Handbook*, Heinemann
- *S/NVQ Level 2 Children's Care, Learning and Development Knowledge and Evidence Resource File*, Heinemann
- *S/NVQ Level 3 Children's Care, Learning and Development Knowledge and Evidence Resource File*, Heinemann

Suggested solutions

Chapter 1

Over to you!

Performance Criteria, page 3

You may have noticed how the Performance Criteria statements define particular aspects of competence that need to be demonstrated by the candidate. They identify specific aims for the candidate, without illustrating how the candidate should do this. For example, Performance Criteria 1 says 'Show children you are paying attention and listening to them'. Each candidate will demonstrate their ability to do this in various ways, such as during a creative activity or when looking at holiday photographs with a child. The important factor here is that the NOS identify key skills, knowledge and understanding; how these are demonstrated will differ from candidate to candidate.

Units, page 5

303 looks at observing and assessing children's and young people's development and planning to promote their development.

305 considers how candidates ensure and protect the rights of children and the importance of promoting children's welfare.

311 considers how to provide leadership within the team, including motivating and supporting them to achieve the objectives of the team and their personal work objective.

326 looks at working with professionals who have the statutory responsibility to keep children safe and protected from abuse or neglect.

Elements, page 5

203.1 Contribute to supporting children's physical development and skills

203.2 Contribute to supporting children's emotional and social development

203.3 Contribute to supporting children's communication and intellectual development

203.4 Contribute to planning for children's development needs

Performance Criteria 2, page 6

1 Communicate with children in a way that is appropriate for their ages, needs and abilities
2 Listen to children and respond to them in a way that shows you value what they say and feel
3 Ask questions, clarify and confirm points
4 Encourage children to ask questions, offer ideas and make suggestions
5 Recognise when there are communication difficulties and adapt the way you communicate accordingly

Knowledge Specifications, page 7

K2D60 Approaches to children that encourage them to participate in activities
K2D69 The effects of security and reassurance on children's confidence
K2H78 Basic information about safe food handling

Removal of italics, page 9

Some of the Performance Criteria address health education and body awareness, which could easily be observed during messy play, toileting, meal times or imaginative play, for example. The candidate might encourage the child to change the dolly's nappy and then wash their hands, discussing the need for hygiene and body awareness during this play.

Where the requirement is adhering to parental wishes and respect for cultural backgrounds, you could observe product evidence, such as the child's personal file or a note from the parent which the candidate is aware of and adhering to, for example.

Key changes, page 11

You will have noticed that the *range specifications* are no longer present in the CCLD NOS. The removal of this detail has allowed candidates and assessors to be more creative and flexible in how they evidence the Performance Criteria. You will notice in other units that some of the details used previously within the range statements have been included in other parts of the NOS. In the EYCE unit there are seven Performance Criteria, but only six in the CCLD unit. In addition to these changes, the language has been made clearer within the CCLD, for example:

EYCE PC1 'Appropriate procedures consistent with the policies of the setting are accurately followed in emergencies'

CCLD PC1 'Remain calm and follow your organisation's procedures for accidents and emergencies, according to your role and responsibility'

EYCE PC7 'All incidents are reported promptly and recorded accurately'

CCLD PC6 'Follow reporting and recording procedures'

The changes in language and presentation make the criteria easier to read and understand for the candidates, allowing them to take ownership of their learning and grow in confidence throughout their training.

Overcoming barriers, page 14

You might have considered pay as an issue within the sector. The childcare sector is notorious for being poorly paid, in relation to the roles and responsibilities of the job. With many childcare settings paying just above minimum wage, practitioners feel that their hard work, commitment and training is not reflected in their pay packet. This can lead to many qualified, experienced and devoted practitioners leaving the sector for alternative employment on the basis of earning a higher income. This then leads to a high turnover within the sector, as practitioners strive to find better paid employment.

You might also have thought about general terms and conditions available to practitioners in the sector. Terms and conditions will vary within the sector, depending upon the setting. For example, teaching assistants may find they are offered term-time only contracts, meaning less annual pay, and less flexibility over holiday arrangements. However, successful management of these issues can support the retention of practitioners. This might be achieved by ensuring that practitioners are clear about their salary and employment terms from the beginning, and that alternative benefits are available, such as training, team building, career progression and job satisfaction. Acknowledgement and appreciation of the practitioner's hard work can make a huge difference to retention, as can motivation, and development of job roles.

You can implement all of these strategies in the training arena. By ensuring that your candidates are fully aware of their roles and responsibilities from the outset, and the commitment required to gain their award, your candidates will feel empowered and informed, thus allowing them to be confident that they have chosen the correct training route for them, and ultimately the appropriate career path. Motivational techniques, team building exercises, acknowledgement of their achievements and recognition of their hard work will all develop their confidence in their abilities to carry out their job roles competently and successfully.

Other barriers to employment include language and cultural issues. Candidates with English as their second language can find it increasingly difficult to get into training, as can men, and people from minority groups.

Under-representation of men, page 14

You might offer the following facts to encourage the young men to consider childcare training as an option that is available to them.

- By promoting a mixed workforce, you can challenge stereotypical assumptions and demonstrate to young children the importance of gender equality. Children may already have a perception of childcare as being 'a woman's job', therefore seeing men in the setting will challenge this thinking.
- Male practitioners can provide role models for young children, particularly where children are brought up without a male role model.
- Male practitioners will bring different experiences to the setting, reflecting their own experiences, backgrounds and cultures. This will further enrich children's experiences and enhance the quality of the childcare provided.
- Employing male practitioners will demonstrate the setting's commitment to anti-discriminatory practice, and exhibit gender diversity.
- Skills shortages will be improved.

Recruiting more men, page 15

Strategies to recruit more men could include:

- campaigns focused on men from black and ethnic minority groups
- targeting areas of high unemployment

- offering taster sessions
- providing childcare support for men who are the main care-givers to their children
- providing men-only courses
- providing male mentors and assessors
- working with employers and Connexions to promote the sector to men
- providing a high level of support
- targeting recruitment more closely to men in local labour markets.

The Common Core, page 19

Sharing this information with your candidates can be done in a variety of ways, from role plays to quizzes. You will decide on how best to disseminate the information, depending on the learning styles of your candidates (more information on learning styles can be found in Chapter 2, page 48). The Common Core fits easily into the S/NVQ, and lends itself to being subject matter within each unit. You might like to ask your candidates to obtain their own copy of the Commom Core as reference to use throughout their training.

Which units?, page 23

1 You might have considered recommending optional unit *210 Support children and young people's play*, as this unit will benefit the candidate in both job roles. Should she want to work with babies in the day nursery, she might want to do *208 Support the development of babies and children under 3* as an extra unit.

2 The most obvious units here would be *307 Promote the healthy and physical development of children, 308 Promote children's well-being and resilience, 321 Support children with disabilities or special educational needs and their families, 325 Support the child or young person's successful transfer and transition in learning and development contexts* and *339 Co-ordinate special educational needs in early education settings.*

3 You might have recommended *306 Plan and organise environments for children and families, 313 Support early intervention for the benefit of children and families, 322 Empower families through the development of parenting skills, 324 Support the delivery of community based services to children and families, 326 Safeguard children from*

harm, *327 Support children who have experienced trauma, 330 Establish and maintain a service for children and families, 331 Support children and families through home visiting* and *334 Deliver services to children and families whose preferred language is not English or Welsh.* You will have noticed that many of the optional units are applicable, and that the candidate should give this a lot of thought before deciding which units to take.

Continuous professional development, page 25

313 Support early intervention for the benefit of children and families

315 Contribute to supporting parents with literacy, numeracy or language needs

319 Promote healthy living for children and families

321 Support children with disabilities or special educational needs and their families

322 Empower families through the development of parenting skills

324 Support the delivery of community based services to children and families

329 Work with a management committee

330 Establish and maintain a service for children and families

331 Support children and families through home visiting

335 Allocate and check work in your team

338 Develop productive working relationships with colleagues

340 Establish, develop and promote quality systems and procedures for the delivery of childcare services

341 Advise and mentor those implementing quality systems and procedures for the delivery of childcare services

342 Meet regulatory requirements in the childcare setting

Skills and knowledge, page 30

1 Communication – during all units of the S/NVQ, particularly 301.

2 Anti-discriminatory practice – during all units of the S/NVQ, particularly 305 and 321.

3 The ability to build relationships – during all units of the S/NVQ, particularly 313, 322 and 324.

Check your understanding, page 34

1 The NOS define the outcomes we expect the candidate to reach.

2 The Level 3 is a nine-unit qualification, comprising of five mandatory units and four optional units. In order to complete the full qualification, the candidate must complete all of the mandatory units, along with the chosen optional units, making up the full award. You will find that the optional units for the Level 3 award are divided into two groups. The candidate must choose two optional units from Group 1 and two optional units from Group 1 or 2.

3 Transitional modules enable candidates to move between the playwork and childcare sectors without having to gain additional full qualifications.

4 An element describes one distinct aspect of the function depicted by the unit. It identifies a particular aspect of the work that the candidate must be able to do.

5 Changes from EYCE to CCLD include the name of the standards, the age range, the removal of range specification and the removal of italics.

6 The role of the Children's Workforce Development Council is to support the development and implementation of local strategies.

7 Under-represented groups within the childcare sector include men and cultural groups.

8 The Common Core of Skills is a set of common, basic skills and knowledge.

9 The table below gives some appropriate job roles at Levels 2 and 3.

Level 2	Level 3
Nursery assistant	Nursery nurse
Crèche worker	Officer in charge
Family support assistant	Family worker
Special needs assistant	Supporting health care professionals
Childminder	Childminder
Playscheme assistant	Playscheme leader

10 The three Principles of the childcare sector are:
- the welfare of the child is paramount
- practitioners contribute to children's care, learning and development and this is reflected in every aspect of practice and service provision
- practitioners work with parents and families who are partners in the care, learning and development of their children and are the child's first and most enduring educators.

Chapter 2

Over to you!

Initial contact, page 41

You might have thought of some of the following questions.

- Where do you see yourself in five years' time?
- Where do you see yourself in ten years' time?
- Tell me about yourself.
- What is your major achievement?
- What do you consider yourself good at doing?
- What sort of person are you?
- What are your strengths?
- What are your areas for improvement.
- How would you approach this training.
- How do you get things done and manage your time?
- How do you manage your day and what other commitments do you have?
- What motivates you?
- How have you changed in the last five years?
- What contribution do you make to a team?
- What would your peers say about you?
- Describe your ideal work environment.
- Describe your worst work environment.
- Do you like to work in a team or on your own?
- What would you do if you weren't able to do this course?
- What do you look forward to most about this course?
- How does the course sound to you?
- Which subjects did you enjoy at school?
- Why do you want to work with children?
- Have you always wanted to work with children?
- What would be your alternative career?
- What do you expect from the training centre?
- What previous experience of childcare do you have?

- What other experience do you have?
- What sort of activities are you interested in outside of work?
- Would your social life infringe on your work commitment?
- Are you a leader or a follower?
- Are you computer literate?
- Do you have any questions to ask me?

Building appropriate relationships, page 43

1 As Emily is confident, you will probably find it easy to build relationships with her. Having enjoyed school and having a supportive family may show you that she doesn't need much input from you. It is important that you develop a trusting relationship with Emily, demonstrating to her that you trust her to come to you with any concerns about her work and that you have an open door. When giving Emily feedback after an assessment, you might ask her how things are going and ensure that she is able to cope with the demands and workload of her training. The relationship should be light and constructive, while allowing Emily the room to develop her own styles and personality. It is important that Emily does not feel she is less important than other candidates who might require more support.

2 You might approach this relationship differently, as you may feel it important to build a relationship with Rani's close family. It might be appropriate to invite Rani's parents into the training centre, perhaps at her interview, or during an open day, to put their minds at rest. Rani may require more support from you to boost her confidence in her abilities, and to grow her self-esteem within her placement. You would ensure that her placement understands the support needs she may have. You might also provide classroom-based activities that demand working in small groups or pairs, in order to support Rani in making new friends within the group.

3 The relationship you build with Paula will need to be strong and definite from the beginning. She may need you to be firm about boundaries. Although she seems very confident, her outgoing personality may be a 'front' for her inner feelings of self-doubt. Her personality seems a little immature, and you will need to demonstrate to her how her behaviour affects others. You should ensure that she is aware that she can discuss issues with you, and that there are support workers available if she needs to talk about her personal problems.

Inclusive assessment opportunities, page 45

Each candidate will need to be supported in different ways. Below are some ideas of how you could support these candidates, and you may well have some ideas of your own.

1 A candidate with a visual impairment may benefit from having their information in a format such as computer disk, large print, email, Braille or audiocassette. Questioning should be done verbally, allowing the candidate to dictate her answers. The placement this candidate attends should be made aware of her needs, and accommodate additional support required. The candidate should be encouraged to talk about her needs to the placement and the children she is working with.

2 It appears that the self-harming was due to the stress caused by the bullying at school. Some people who self-harm will find it helpful to talk to someone. This could be a friend or family member, but it might also be a professional: a youth worker, a doctor or nurse, a social worker, a teacher or a counsellor, for example. You should ensure that the candidate feels confident to talk to you and let you know if she feels the need to self-harm again, and introduce her to your centre's support worker or counsellor, who could help the candidate with any underlying issues she might still face.

3 Some candidates with dyslexia may experience high levels of stress, especially when disclosing this information to you for the first time during an interview. They may also find it difficult to answer questions when feeling under pressure. With this in mind, the interview should be conducted in a friendly and informal manner, to put the candidate at ease. Should the candidate have to sit tests as part of the interview, it may be necessary to allow them extra time to complete them. People with dyslexia may also have difficulty finding their way round an unfamiliar environment, so you should arrange a specific place to meet them, sending directions and a map, along with a number you can be contacted on.

Methods of differentiation, page 47

You might have thought about how you planned activities that could easily be made simpler or harder for the children to complete. For example, you might have had a jigsaw table with a range of jigsaws at varying degrees of difficulty. You might have considered how you adapted your plans for a child with a particular need, or made an activity more challenging for a gifted child. Whatever adjustments you have thought about, they will have been planned in advance, being fed from your knowledge of that individual child, and their capabilities, interests and personality. All of this is transferable into adult learning. By knowing your candidates' interests, skills, abilities and personalities, you can plan their learning accordingly and use their knowledge to differentiate their learning either in the classroom or in the placement.

Strategies to engage different learning styles, page 49

Some ways you might engage different learning styles include the following.

- Split candidates into groups of similar levels, working on individual tasks within each group.
- Split candidates into groups with a higher-ability candidate in each group.
- Encourage candidates to work in small groups/pairs, or individually, and then feed back and compare results.
- Enable learners to self-check (by giving answer sheets) or mark each other's work.
- Have different activities/tasks in different parts of the room. Candidates should be encouraged to choose which one to do, or work round them one by one at their own pace. You can then intervene where appropriate, to support or advise.
- If you are providing your candidates with worksheets, you might find it useful to have different ones according to level. You might find it helps to ask the candidates to choose the level they want to start at and progress through them at their own rate. This will provide you with an excellent opportunity to assess the confidence candidates have in their own abilities, or observe how particular candidates support others.
- Have resources that cater for different learning styles.
- Use everyday objects wherever possible.
- Allow candidates to work and access information in their own time and using their preferred learning style.
- Use open-ended activities and questioning.
- Ask candidates to plan their own lessons and activities.
- Encourage candidates to talk about their learning and discoveries with their peers and the rest of the cohort.
- Encourage candidates to reflect on their learning and practice.
- Offer choices and extension activities for the more able candidates.

Activities for differentiation, pages 54–56

The activities provided within the sheet are diverse in their ability to work with a range of people with differing learning styles. For example, activities 6 and 11 encourage the use of discussion within small and large groups, which is valuable to auditory learners, while activity 13 works around role play, which is ideal for kinaesthetic learners. Good assessors will be able to make links between the learning styles of their candidates and the types of activity that will enhance the learning opportunities available to their candidates.

Check your understanding, page 56

1 Trust, respect and honesty
2 The control of the spread of information that it is inappropriate to disseminate or share
3 The Data Protection Act 1998
4 To enable the learning you provide to be tailored to the individual's needs, and to understand how their prior learning experiences have affected the way they envisage their new learning to take place
5 It sets out guidelines for access to assessment, detailing how all candidates should be offered appropriate support to enable them to access assessment.
6 Easy access, translators available, hearing loop system fitted (among others)
7 Taking action to counter discrimination, identifying and challenging discrimination
8 The matching of work to the differing capabilities of individuals or groups of pupils in order to extend their learning
9 To ensure that all candidates are treated as individuals, and with equal concern
10 By listening, seeing and doing – all of the different types of learning, mixed together

Chapter 3

Over to you!

Questioning candidates, page 68

Depending on what you actually saw the candidate achieve, you might ask some of the following questions. You might also have thought of some of your own.

- What safety precautions should you consider when bottle-feeding a baby?
- How might you support a breast-feeding mother within the setting?
- How would you ensure that the child's carer was aware of how the baby had been fed throughout the day?
- What are the storage and handling regulations for milk feeds, including breast-milk?
- How would you avoid cross-contamination and cross-infection?

Witness testimonies, page 69

This witness testimony provides evidence for the following Performance Criteria.

Unit	Element	PC
CCLD 201 Contribute to positive relationships	**CCLD 201.1** Interact with and respond to children	**2** Use a considerate and sympathetic approach whilst paying attention and listening to children
	CCLD 201.2 Interact with and respond to adults	**3** Respond confidently, in a way which shows you have listened to their views with care and attention
	CCLD 201.3 Communicate with children	**1** Communicate clearly, in ways that the child will understand
CCLD 202 Help to keep children safe	**CCLD 202.1** Prepare and maintain a safe environment	**5** Supervise children's safety appropriately and consistently, according to their ages, needs and abilities
		6 Encourage children to be aware of personal safety and the safety of others
	CCLD 202.2 Follow procedures for accidents, emergencies and illness	**1** Remain calm and follow your organisation's procedures for accidents and emergencies, according to your role and responsibility
		3 Maintain the safety of the people involved
		4 Provide reassurance and comfort to the people involved
		6 Follow reporting and recording procedures

Expert witnesses, page 70

It is essential that where expert witnesses are used to provide evidence for candidates' portfolios, records of their achievements, experience and professional development are kept up to date. You might like to keep a file for each witness that contains:

- name, address and contact details
- curriculum vitae
- copies of certificates, with originals available for the external verifier on the external verification visit
- up-to-date continuous professional development, details of courses attended and updates, etc. to prove occupational competence
- records of attendance at standardisation meetings.

Written evidence, page 70

There are many different projects you could set for this knowledge specification. The following is just one example.

Produce a resource for other workers in a Children's Centre that can be used as a quick reference guide to developmental processes from birth to 16 years. In your research, use a range of books and the internet to ensure you get a thorough range of information. Remember to correctly identify the sources that you have used.

The presentation of your work is important. The resource should clearly identify progression of skills.

The categories of age you should research and reference are:

- 0–1 years
- 1–3 years
- 4–5 years
- 6–7 years
- 8–12 years
- 13–16 years.

The areas of development should include:

- physical
- communication
- intellectual/cognitive
- personal
- social
- emotional
- behavioural.

This activity has been taken from a selection within the *S/NVQ Level 3 Children's Care, Learning and Development Knowledge and Evidence Resource*, published by Heinemann.

Reflective accounts, page 71

Dave's reflective account is very short and basic, although he has set the scene well, and the reader has a mental picture of what is happening. You might advise Dave to think about putting more detail in, such as why he chose those particular captains, and how the other children reacted to being picked in this way. Dave should also be supported in reflecting on his practice. Which parts of the activity were successful, and which parts not so successful? How might Dave do this activity differently if he were to do it again? Dave should also think about his role within the group, and consider whether he could have played a more active part in the activity. Giving more detail about the upset child will demonstrate whether Dave's response was appropriate. Dave should then be encouraged to think about how this activity has helped him to develop his skills and how this will impact on his practice in the future.

Planning assessment opportunities, page 77

Assessment Plan

Award: .... **Date:** ....

Candidate's Name: A. Candidate.......... **Candidate PIN No:** ....

Assessor's Name: Ann Assessor.........

Evidence to be gathered	Date	By whom	Achieved
Holistic observation within the nursery setting			
Professional discussion on language development			
Witness testimony on supporting children's exercise			
Reflective account on creative play			
Written questioning on theories of play			

Check your understanding, page 85

1 Direct observation, expert witness testimonies, professional discussion

2 Name, address and contact details, CV, copies of certificates, up-to-date CPD (Continuing Professional Development), details of courses attended and updates and records of attendance at standardisation meetings

3 Examples could include the following.
- Choose the right time.
- Start with positive comments.
- Encourage self-assessment.
- Draw attention to and reinforce strengths, as well as areas for improvement.
- Ask questions rather than making statements.
- Be specific, giving explicit examples.
- Refer to behaviour that can be changed.
- Demonstrate what should and could be done to improve.
- Set deadlines and targets for improvement.
- Be descriptive rather than evaluative.
- Ensure the candidate fully understands what is being discussed.

4 Why and how questions

5 To check your candidate's understanding

6 A witness who was present at the time an activity took place

7 Planning will provide your candidates with a clear sense of direction and enable them to assess their own progress. Careful planning will also help you to meet the individual needs of your candidates, and understand how best to support them through their training.

8 Examples could include the following.
- Ensure that assessment is focused on the needs of the individual candidate.
- Set measurable goals so that achievement of candidates can be assessed.
- Specify learning goals and targets that can be measured and assessed.
- Provide candidates with a sense of direction, and a focus.
- Provide a tool for motivation as candidates see their training progressing.

9 **Initial assessment** assesses starting levels and identifies appropriate learning opportunities, whereas **diagnostic screening** identifies skills and weaknesses to inform the Individual Learning Plan.

Chapter 4

Over to you!

Using a range of assessment methods, page 90

The term 'using a range of assessment methods' means assessing your candidate's competence using the assessment opportunities you looked at in Chapter 4. These might be:

- direct observation
- oral and written questions
- witness testimony
- expert witness evidence
- case studies, projects and assignments
- reflective accounts
- professional discussion
- work products
- simulation
- accreditation of prior learning.

A1.1 Develop plans for assessing competence with candidates, page 94

The evidence requirements for unit A1.1 are:

1 three assessment plans for a minimum of two different candidates
2 one record of a written or spoken explanation
3 two written outcomes from progress reviews.

Assessment plans, page 95

Your assessment plan may look something like this, or you may have some ideas of your own. The main concern is that the plan should cover the assessment of the complete unit using a minimum of four assessment methods, one of which is direct observation, and should demonstrate how others have been involved in the assessment process. The following plan demonstrates six assessment methods, including observation of the candidate, and shows the involvement of the candidate's line manager and first aider to support the evidence.

Assessment Plan

Award: CCLD L3	**Date:** 14ᵗʰ September 2005
Candidate's Name: Jackie Simpson	**Candidate PIN No:** 05/245363
Assessor's Name: T. Assessor	**Unit/Element:** 302

Evidence	Element reference	Knowledge specification reference	By whom	By when
Direct observation of Jackie working with babies during day-to-day routine, focusing on health and safety within the setting	302.1, PCs 1, 2, 3 302.2, PCs 2, 4, 5	K3H190 K3H191 K3D195	JS TA	24/09/05
Professional discussion focusing on record keeping e.g. risk assessment, hazards and security procedures – see discussion plan	302.1, PCs 1, 4, 5, 6 302.2, PCs 1, 3	K3P189 K3H192 K3H193 K3H194 K3D195 K3H196 K3H200	JS TA	26/09/05
Witness testimony regarding how Jackie has implemented and followed H&S procedures of the setting from Jackie's line manager	302.2, PCs 1, 2, 3, 6	K3H201 K3H264 K3S198	Lisa Jones	26/09/05
Reflective account on safety during outings	302.2, PCs 6, 7	K3H192	JS	26/09/05
APL: First Aid certificate	302.3, PCs 1, 2, 3, 4, 5, 6	K3H197 K3S198 K3H199	JS	26/09/05
Witness testimony from designated first aider focusing on Jackie's responses to accidents, illness and other injuries	302.3, PCs 1, 2, 3, 4, 5, 6	K3H193 K3H196 K3H197 K3S198 K3H199 K3H200	Maureen Blakely	26/09/05

A1.2 Judge evidence against criteria to make assessment decisions, page 97

The evidence requirements for unit A1.2 are:

1 three assessment decision records
2 a record of a professional discussion.

Assessment decision records, page 97

The plan identifies six opportunities for assessment for this candidate. A1.2 requires you to show the decisions you have made based on the assessments planned. Therefore you might submit a copy of the direct observation of Jackie working with babies during the day-to-day routine, focusing on health and safety within the setting. At the end of this observation, you will have made an assessment decision as to the competency of your candidate and given her feedback on this decision. You might include a copy of the professional discussion, demonstrating your ability to make an assessment decision by providing feedback to the candidate and cross-referencing this with the NOS.

Occupational competence, page 103

Your table may contain some of the following ideas, or you may have more of your own.

Unit	Assessor's possible previous job role/experience	Ways to maintain competence
CCLD 309 – Plan and implement curriculum frameworks for early education	• Nursery nurse in early years unit within a school • Primary school teacher curriculum leader	• Attending training on curriculum frameworks • Work-shadowing curriculum manager at nursery school
CCLD 315 – Contribute to supporting parents with literacy, numeracy and language needs	• Family Centre worker • Family support worker • Tutor of English for speakers of other languages (ESOL)	• Researching family learning opportunities, and working alongside practitioners • Work-shadowing ESOL tutor
CCLD 316 – Maintain and develop a childminding business	• Childminder • Introduction to Childminding Practice tutor (ICP)	• Spending time with childminder in their own home • Attending ICP training
CCLD 321 – Support children with disabilities or special educational needs and their families	• Special educational needs (SEN) co-ordinator • Nanny to child with special needs • Nursery nurse in special needs school • Family support worker	• Attending specialist training • Working in special educational support unit • Work-shadowing family support worker
CCLD 336 – Contribute to childcare practice in group living	• Social worker • Residential childcare worker • Playworker	• Attending training on group living • Work-shadowing residential social worker
CCLD 345 – Help pupils to develop their literacy skills	• Teacher • Support tutor • Classroom support worker	• Spending time in classroom environment
CCLD 327 – Support children who have experienced trauma	• Family support worker • Asylum/refugee support worker • Social worker – domestic violence	• Spending time with organisations who support children and families who have experienced trauma

Check your understanding, pages 111–112

1 No, the A1 covers the content of the A2; however, if you have the A2, you may want to do the A1.

2 You might be involved in:
- developing learning plans
- demonstrating your understanding of the NOS
- planning assessment opportunities and processes
- supporting candidates with differing and/or additional needs
- finding out about differing assessment methods
- providing candidates with feedback
- recording assessment decisions
- working with others involved in the assessment process.

3 Four

4 Two

5 If you only wish to assess candidates through observation

6 Your assessor might cover the following questions.
- Was the feedback given to the candidate at an appropriate place and time?
- Was the candidate given advice on how to prove their competence and how to develop the necessary skills or provide further evidence?
- Were you able to identify and agree the next steps in the assessment process and how this will be achieved?

7 From the Employment National Training Organisation (ENTO)

8 To ensure that standards are being met coherently and consistently within all training centres

9 Reviewing the quality of the assessment decision once the assessor has confirmed the unit/portfolio is complete

10 To ensure that everyone involved in the award is aware of the requirements of the NOS and will work to the same standards of assessment

Chapter 5

Check your understanding, page 122

1 A reflective practitioner is a person who thinks critically, analysing their actions with the goal of changing and improving occupational practice.

2 To ensure that you are aware of changes in legislation and standards and evaluate your performance against best practice benchmarks

3 By listening to feedback from colleagues, line managers and candidates

4 You might implement new ideas and practices that will encourage colleagues to come out of their comfort zones and move forward.

5 As your practice, knowledge and skills develop through reflective practice, your candidates will reap the benefits of a more confident and knowledgeable assessor.

6 Monitor processes, practices and outcomes from work, evaluate own performance using best practice benchmarks, share reflections with others and use their feedback

7 Experiences, ideas and understanding; reflection and re-evaluation; outcome, better practice and application

Glossary

Accreditation of Prior Learning (APL) Identifying candidates' previous learning experiences and referencing them accordingly to the NOS

Anti-discriminatory practice Taking action to counter discrimination, identifying and challenging discrimination

Best practice benchmarks Standards that are widely agreed as providing the most advanced, up-to-date thinking and practice against which you can measure what you are doing (not minimum standards). They may be statutory/regulatory or based on other requirements or research

Case studies, projects and assignments Used to provide evidence where no naturally occurring evidence is available

Closed question A question that can be answered with either a single word or a short phrase, such as 'Yes' or 'No'

Cohort A group of individuals having a factor in common

Competency Having the necessary skill or knowledge to do something successfully

Confidentiality The control of the spread of information that is inappropriate to disseminate or share

Diagnostic screening Identifies skills and weaknesses to inform the Individual Learning Plan (ILP)

Differentiation There are many different definitions of differentiation. Ofsted defines it as 'the matching of work to the differing capabilities of individuals or groups of pupils in order to extend their learning'

Direct observation A record of the actions performed by the candidate during real-work situations

Element Describes one distinct aspect of the function depicted by the unit. Identifies one particular aspect of the work that the candidate must be able to do

Expert witness An approved practitioner, inducted by the training centre, who carries out observations on the candidate in order to provide written evidence

Holistic assessment Observing real-work situations as they happen with a view to covering a range of units and elements

Inclusion   Identifying, understanding and breaking down barriers to participation and belonging

Individual Learning Plan (ILP)   A flexible tool that is used by the assessor to assess candidates' accomplishments and/or needs in essential knowledge, skills and abilities

Initial assessment   Assesses starting levels and identifies appropriate learning opportunities

Inter-agency working   A range of agencies working together to achieve more outcomes than if working in isolation

Interim sampling   Reviewing the quality of the assessment at various stages within the assessment process

Knowledge Specification   Describes what is necessary for the candidate to know and understand in order to be competent in a variety of work contexts and at different times. This forms the foundation for each unit. Without this knowledge the candidate cannot prove competence

Minority group   A secondary group whose members have significantly less control or power over their lives than members of a dominant or majority group

Occupational competence   Having held a post for a minimum of one year within the last two years that involved performing the activities defined in the standards as an experienced practitioner. *OR* Being an experienced trainer or instructor of at least one year's standing in the competence area of the standards

Open question   A question that allows a longer answer, giving the candidate control of the conversation

Performance Criteria   Describe one distinct aspect of the function depicted by the unit. Identify a particular aspect of the work that the candidate must be able to do

Product evidence   Products derived from real-work situations, such as fire drill records, accident books, stationery orders, etc.

Professional discussion   A discussion between the candidate and the assessor to draw depth and breadth of knowledge and understanding and establish the rationale behind the candidate's actions

Quality assurance   A system under which an assessment team ensures that all services are of high quality and will satisfy the integrity of the award

Questioning   Using questions to clarify the knowledge and understanding of the candidate

Reflective account   A written or oral account by the candidate reflecting on their practice

Reflective practice   The process of thinking about and critically analysing your actions with the goal of changing and improving occupational practice

Simulation   Setting up an observation that is not within a real-work situation. Only to be used where clearly indicated within the NOS

Summative sampling   Reviewing the quality of the assessment decision once the assessor has confirmed the unit/portfolio is complete

Unit   Describes a particular function within a job and breaks it down to list the specific activities or duties this comprises. Indicates the functions that the candidate is required to carry out in the workplace, forming the building blocks that make up the qualification

Witness testimony   An account of a candidate's performance, written by someone other than the candidate's assessor

Work products   Evidence produced by the candidate themselves during work practice

S/NVQ ASSESSOR HANDBOOK for CCLD

INDEX

A1 award 87–112
  action plan 90–1
  assessment decision records 97
  assessment methods 90, 94
  changes from D-units 88
  external verifier 108
  four elements 4, 5, 92
  independent assessors 107
  internal verifier 107, 109–10, 111
  judging evidence against criteria 97
  knowledge requirements 92–3
  personnel involved 101
  professional discussion 97, 99
  progress reviews 96
  providing feedback and support 98–9
  structure of 88–9
  written or spoken explanation 96
  your assessor 106
  your candidates 104
  see also unit
A2 award 90, 100, 101
  changes from D-units 88
  structure of 88–9
  see also unit
ACCAC 109
access to assessment 44–7
accreditation of prior learning (APL) 72–3
action plan for A1 award 90–1
activities
  for differentiation 50–6
  group 53, 54, 55
  notes sheet 54–6
Administer Provision within Childcare
  Setting (unit 328) 150–1
Advise and Mentor those Implementing
  Quality Systems (unit 341) 157
age range 2, 8, 9–10
Allocate and Check Work in your Team
  (unit 335) 154
anti-discriminatory practice 44
APL 72–3

Assess Children's Progress According to
  Curriculum Frameworks (unit 310)
  139–40
assessment
  access to 44–7
  methods 90, 94
  reviews after 76–7
  standardising 110
  verifying 110
assessment opportunities
  planning for 57, 73–7
  range available 58–73
assessment plans 64, 77, 125
  A1 award 93–6
  A2 award 100
assessors
  for A1 award 106
  benefits of e-portfolios 82
  requirements 101–4
  see also A1 award
assignments as evidence 70
auditory learning style 48
authenticity of evidence 78

best practice 32
  benchmarks 3, 117, 135
body language 67

candidates
  and A1 award 104
  individual needs of 75, 104
Care for Children at Home (unit 320) 146
career pathways 22–3, 31
  assessors 89
case study activities 53, 54
case study evidence 70
centres: benefits of e-portfolios 82
child protection certificate 149
childminding unit 103, 143–4
Children and Young People's Plan 13
Children's Care, Learning and Development
  (CCLD) 1, 2–3, 123

benefits of 2
changes from EYCE 8–11
imported units 11
links between Common Core 20–1
structure of 3–4
see also Level 2; Level 3; unit
Children's Centres 24, 25, 136, 143
   multi-agency approach 28–9
Children's Workforce Development
      Strategy 1, 12–31, 43
closed questions 66
cloze activities 54, 56
Co-ordinate Special Educational Needs
      (unit 339) 156
co-ordinating assessor 106
coaching 158
colleagues, working with 116, 118
collecting evidence 57
   see also evidence
Common Assessment Framework 24
Common Core of Skills and
      Knowledge 18–22
   areas of expertise 18
   links with CCLD 20–1
communication, effective 21
competence 2–3, 32
   assessment of 57, 58
confidence of candidates 80
confidentiality 32, 72
   of candidates' information 37
   and children's records 36
   expert witness evidence 69–70
   and observation 98
   in professional relationships 36–8
   in units 132, 142, 144, 148, 152, 156
   when to breach 37
consistency of performance 78
continuous professional development
      25, 105
Contribute to Childcare Practice in Group
      Living (unit 336) 103, 154–5
Contribute to Effectiveness of Teams
      (unit 207) 131
Contribute to Positive Relationships (unit 201)
      20, 127

Contribute to Supporting Parents with Literacy,
      Numeracy or Language Needs (unit 315)
      103, 143
Create Environments that Promote Positive
      Behaviour (unit 337) 155
creative activities 51
cross-referencing 60–2
currency of evidence 78

D-units and new units 88
Data Protection Act (1998) 36, 44
Deliver Services to Children and Families
      whose Preferred Language is not
      English or Welsh (unit 334) 154
Develop and Maintain a Healthy, Safe and
      Secure Environment (unit 302) 21, 134
Develop Productive Working Relationships
      with Colleagues (unit 338) 155–6
Develop and Promote Positive Relationships
      (unit 301) 21, 133–4
development of children 20, 22
diagnostic screening 75
differentiation between candidates 47–56
   activities for 50–6
   categories of 47
   methods of 47
   types of need 48
direct observation 59–63, 124–6
   cross-referencing 60–2
   Unit 201 127
Disability Discrimination Act (1995) 44
disabled candidates 44, 45
discrimination 17, 44
discussion
   activities 54
   lead professional topics 27
   see also professional discussion
diversity 31
   of candidates 43–5
   in workforce 17

e-portfolios 81–4
   advantages of 82–3
   OneFile 84
early years professional (EYP) 24–5, 26
elements of A1 award 4, 5

Empower Families through Development of Parenting Skills (unit 322) 147
empowering candidates 41
Enable Individual Learning through Coaching (unit 344) 158
English as second language 45
essays and assignments 51
Establish, Develop and Promote Quality Systems (unit 340) 156–7
Establish and Maintain a Service for Children and Families (unit 330) 151–52
Every Child Matters 18, 22, 147
evidence
    gathering 57, 58–9
    judging 78
    written 70–1
    recording 63, 65–6
    see also individual units; unit
experimental activities 53
expert witness evidence 69–70
    in Level 2 units 129, 132
    in Level 3 units 134, 135, 139, 140, 141, 142, 143, 144, 145, 147, 148, 149, 150, 152, 154, 157
external agencies 116
external verifier 108
EYCE, changes from 8–11, 127

feedback and reflective practice 121, 135
feedback to candidates 78–81
    A1 award requirements 98–9
    benefits of 78
    good practice 79, 81
first aid training 134, 142
formative tests 52

goals and targets 75, 76–7
group discussion 54
group work 50

health and safety 21, 22
Help Pupils Develop their Literacy Skills (unit 345) 103, 158–9
Help Pupils Develop their Numeracy Skills (unit 346) 159
Help to Keep Children Safe (unit 202) 20, 127–8

holistic assessment 59, 60, 127, 130
holistic observation 8, 127, 129
    in units 130, 133, 137, 138, 141, 142, 146, 147, 151, 155, 156, 158

ICT unit (323) 148
imported units 11
inclusion and assessment 45
independent assessors 107
Individual Learning Plans (ILPs) 74–5
    purpose and use 75
information and confidentiality 38
information sharing 21
initial assessment 75
initial contact with candidates 40–1
integrated working 29
inter-agency working 28–9
interim sampling 110
internal verification
    and A1 assessors 106
    benefits of e-portfolios 82
    contributing towards 90
    policies 110
    principles for evidence 78
internal verifier
    quality and standardisation 109–10, 111
    role of 107, 109–10
    V2 award 88
interviews with candidates 40
    with additional needs 45
Involve Families in Childcare Setting (unit 332) 153

job roles: Levels 2 and 3 23
judging evidence 78
    see also evidence

kinaesthetic learning style 48, 50, 51
knowledge requirements: A1 award 92–3
Knowledge Specifications 6–7
    links to Common Core 22
    numbering 7, 22

lead professional 24, 26
    possible discussion topics 27
    skills and knowledge required 27
leadership, promoting 30–1
learning, planning candidates' 116

learning styles 48–9, 51, 96
Level 2 award 124
  links between units 131, 132
  possible job roles 23
Level 3 award 124
  links between units 137, 139, 140, 141, 142,
    143, 146, 150, 151, 153, 154, 156, 157, 158
  possible job roles 23

Maintain and Develop a Childminding Business
    (unit 316) 103, 143–4
male under-representation 14–16
mandatory units 3
Meet Regulatory Requirements (unit 342) 157
Men into Childcare Project 16
mentoring 158
minority groups 16–17
monitoring practice 110
motivation of candidates
  and e-portfolios 82, 83
  ILPs 75
multi-agency working 20, 21, 22, 28–9, 31
  Children's Centres 28–9
  DfES toolkits 29
multi-disciplinary working 12, 31
multi-sensory learning style 48

needs of candidates 75, 104, 116
  additional 43–7
NPQICL 31
NVQ in CCLD see Children's Care, Learning
    and Development
NVQ Code of Practice 109

observation of candidates 98–9, 124
  and consent 141, 145, 146, 152, 153, 156
  direct 59–63
  evidence for units 128, 131, 135, 136, 137,
    138, 139, 140, 144, 145, 146, 148, 151,
    152, 153, 154, 155, 156, 158
  see also holistic observation
occupational competence 102–4
  maintaining 103–4
occupational practice 22
OneFile portfolio assessment 84
open questioning 50, 66
optional units 2, 3–4

performance criteria 3, 5–6
plan, assessment 64
Plan and Implement Curriculum Frameworks
    (unit 309) 103, 138–9
Plan and Implement Positive Environments
    (unit 312) 140–41
Plan and Organise Environments for Children
    and Families (unit 306) 136–7
Plan for and Support Self-directed Play
    (unit 318) 144–5
planning for assessing competence 93–6
planning for assessment opportunities 73–7
  benefits of 74
  setting goals and targets 75, 76–7
playwork: males in workforce 14
portfolios 57, 58
  e-portfolios 81–4
  working file 72
positive relationships unit 127
practical activities 53
Prepare and Maintain Environments (unit 205)
    20, 129–30
presentations 53
Principles and Values 1, 31–3, 101
product evidence 8, 63, 145
  in units 148, 149, 151, 152, 153,
    154, 155, 156, 157, 158
professional discussion 63–6, 92, 97, 99, 100
  Level 2 units 128, 129, 131, 132, 133
  Level 3 units 134, 135, 136, 137, 138, 139,
    140, 142–4, 146, 147, 148, 149, 150, 151,
    152, 153, 154, 155, 157, 158
  planning 63–4
  recording and evidencing 63, 65–6
progress reviews 96
project evidence 70
Promote Children's Development
    (unit 303) 21, 134–5
Promote Children's Well-being and Resilience
    (unit 308) 138
Promote Health and Physical Development of
    Children (unit 307) 137–8
Promote Healthy Living (unit 319) 145
Protect and Promote Children's Rights
    (unit 305) 21, 136

Provide Leadership for your Team
(unit 311) 140
Provide Physical Care that Promotes Health
and Development (unit 314) 142

quality assurance 90, 108–10
A1 award requirements 99
quality schemes 108–9
questioning 66–8, 129
as unit evidence 136, 146
verbal 67–8
quizzes 52

realistic evidence 78
recording evidence 63, 65–6
records and confidentiality 36
Recruit, Select and Keep Colleagues
(unit 333) 153
recruitment of practitioners 13
male 14–16
Reflect on and Develop Practice
(unit 304) 21, 135
reflection-in-action 115
reflective accounts 71
as Level 2 evidence 129, 133
as Level 3 evidence 134, 135, 137,
140, 145, 155
reflective practice 21, 113–22
and assessment reviews 76
challenging existing practice 120
checklist 121
and constructive feedback 80
developing skills of 114, 117–18
developing your work 116
on knowledge-in-practice 115
and moving forward 118
questioning actions 115
questioning candidates 67
relationships 42–3
building effective 35, 36–43
with candidates 38, 39–41, 56
positive 20, 21
reliability of evidence 78
research activities 54, 56
retaining workforce 18–27
reviews after assessments 76–7

Safeguard Children from Harm
(unit 326) 149–50
safeguarding children 20, 21, 22
sampling of assessment 110
Schon, Donald 115
Sector Skills Council 13
self-assessment 135
self-esteem of candidates 80
SENCO unit 156
simulation 72, 142
social exclusion 16–17
standardisation of assessment 111
standardisation meetings 102, 107, 108, 111
stereotyping 17
sufficiency of evidence 78
summative sampling 110
supplementary evidence 58
Support a Child with Disabilities or SEN
(unit 209) 132–3
Support Children with Disabilities or SEN
(unit 321) 103, 146–7
Support Children and Families through Home
Visiting (unit 331) 152
Support Children who Have Experienced
Trauma (unit 327) 103, 150
Support Children and Young People's Play
(unit 210) 133
Support Children's Development
(unit 203) 20, 128–9
Support Children's Play and Learning (unit 206)
20, 130
Support the Delivery of Community Based
Services (unit 324) 148
Support Development of Babies and Children
(unit 208) 131–2
Support Early Intervention (unit 313) 141–2
Support Learners by Mentoring
(unit 343) 158
support needs of candidates see needs
Support the Young Person's Successful Transfer
and Transition (unit 325) 149
SVQ in CCLD 123
see also Children's Care, Learning and
Development
SWOT analysis 39

taped evidence 65–6
terminology of NOS CCLD 11
time allocation to candidates 42
transitions, supporting 20, 22, 149
travellers 16, 17
trust and relationships 36, 37, 39, 40, 42

unit 201 20, 127
unit 202 20, 127–8
unit 203 20, 128–9
unit 204 20, 129
unit 205 20, 129–30
unit 206 20, 130
unit 207 131
unit 208 131–2
unit 209 132–3
unit 210 133
unit 301 21, 133–4
unit 302 21, 134
unit 303 21, 134–5
unit 304 21, 135
unit 305 21, 136
unit 306 136–7
unit 307 137–8
unit 308 138
unit 309 138–9
unit 310 139–40
unit 311 140
unit 312 140–41
unit 313 141–2
unit 314 142
unit 315 143
unit 316 143–4
unit 317 144
unit 318 144–5
unit 319 145
unit 320 146
unit 321 146–7
unit 322 147
unit 323 148
unit 324 148
unit 325 149
unit 326 149–50
unit 327 150
unit 328 150–1

unit 329 151
unit 330 151–2
unit 331 152
unit 332 153
unit 333 153
unit 334 154
unit 335 154
unit 336 154–5
unit 337 155
unit 338 155–6
unit 339 156
unit 340 156–7
unit 341 157
unit 342 157
unit 343 158
unit 344 158
unit 345 158–9
unit 346 159
Use Information and Communication
    Technology (unit 323) 148
Use Support to Develop own Practice
    (unit 204) 20, 129

V1 and V2 awards 88
validity of evidence 78
Values 31–2
    see also Principles and Values
verification see internal verification
visual learning style 48, 50, 51

witness evidence 68–70
    in units 128, 139, 141, 153
witness status list 68
Work with Families to Enhance Children's
    Learning and Development (unit 317)
    144
Work with a Management Committee
    (unit 329) 151
work products 63, 72
workforce
    development 12–31
    males in 14–16
    retaining 18–27
worksheets 52
written evidence 70–1

S/NVQ Levels 2 and 3 Children's Care, Learning and Development: Optional Units Online

The flexibility you need with extra resources available to download from our website

- ◆ Written and designed with the same easy-to-use layout as the Candidate Handbooks, to be downloaded in PDF format.

- ◆ Enable easy access to optional units not covered in the Candidate Handbooks.

- ◆ Provide valuable extra content for colleges and Training providers to add to their VLE for candidates to access.

- ◆ Two-tier pricing ensures excellent value for both individual candidates (single-use version) and colleges/training providers (multiple-use version).

- ◆ Visit www.harcourt.co.uk/childcare to order.

Visit your local bookshop, go to www.harcourt.co.uk/childcare, or contact our Customer Services team on 01865 888118 for further information.

Sign up for the FREE Childcare eNewsletter at www.harcourt.co.uk/vocnews.

S/NVQ Level 2 Children's Care, Learning and Development

Unit 210: Support children and young people's play
Single-use version: 978 0 435462 03 1
Multiple-use version: 978 0 435462 04 8

S/NVQ Level 3 Children's Care, Learning and Development

Unit 311: Provide leadership for your team
Single-use version: 978 0 435463 79 3
Multiple-use version: 978 0 435 463 80 9

Unit 314: Provide physical care that promotes the health and development of babies and children under 3 years
Single-use version: 978 0 435463 77 9
Multiple-use version: 978 0 435 463 78 6

Unit 316: Maintain and develop a childminding business
Single-use version: 978 0 435463 75 5
Multiple-use version: 978 0 435463 76 2

Unit 320: Care for children at home
Single-use version: 978 0 435463 73 1
Multiple-use version: 978 0 435463 74 8

 01865 888118    01865 314029    orders@harcourt.co.uk    www.harcourt.co.uk

M455

S/NVQ Children's Care, Learning and Development: Knowledge and Evidence Resource Files with CD-ROMs

Complete tutor and assessor support for the 2005 S/NVQ at Levels 2 and 3

◆ Each Knowledge and Evidence Resource File provides valuable support for tutors and assessors, including photocopiable activities for delivering and assessing underpinning knowledge, an introduction to the new standards and recording documentation.

◆ Written by a team of experienced tutors and assessors to ensure the best possible support and resources are available.

◆ The CD-ROMs contain additional resources, including PowerPoint presentations and fact sheets to help with the delivery of key topics.

◆ All material in the files is photocopiable and is also provided on the accompanying CD-ROM for you to customise and print.

S/NVQ Level 2 Children's Care, Learning and Development: Knowledge and Evidence Resource File with CD-ROM 978 0 435449 18 6	S/NVQ Level 3 Children's Care, Learning and Development: Knowledge and Evidence Resource File with CD-ROM 978 0 435449 20 9

Visit your local bookshop, go to <u>www.harcourt.co.uk/childcare</u>, or contact our Customer Services team on 01865 888118 for further information.

Sign up for the FREE Childcare eNewsletter at <u>www.harcourt.co.uk/vocnews</u>.